33 things every girl should know about women's story

33 things every girl should know about
women's history

FROM SUFFRAGETTES
TO SKIRT LENGTHS
TO THE E.R.A.
edited by TONYA BOLDEN

CROWN PUBLISHERS
NEW YORK

Published in the United States by Crown Publishers, an imprint of Random House
Children's Books, a division of Random House, Inc., New York.

Acknowledgments for permission to reprint previously published material can be found
on pages 230 and 231.

Picture acknowledgments can be found on page 232.

CROWN and colophon are trademarks of Random House, Inc.

www.randomhouse.com/teens

Educators and librarians, for a variety of teaching tools, visit us at
www.randomhouse.com/teachers

Library of Congress Cataloging-in-Publication Data

Bolden, Tonya.
33 things every girl should know about women's history: from suffragettes to skirt
lengths to the E.R.A. / edited by Tonya Bolden.—1st ed.

p. cm.

SUMMARY: Uses poems, essays, letters, photographs and more to present the actions
and achievements of women in the United States, from its beginnings up through the
twentieth century. Includes index.
ISBN-10: 0-375-91122-7 (lib. bdg.) — ISBN-10: 0-375-81122-2 (trade pbk.)
ISBN-13: 978-0-375-91122-4 (lib. bdg.) — ISBN-13: 978-0-375-81122-7 (trade pbk.)

1. Women—United States—History—Juvenile literature. 2. Feminism—United States—
History—Juvenile literature. 3. Women's rights—United States—History—Juvenile litera-
ture. [1. Women—History. 2. Women's rights—History. 3. Feminism—History.]
I. Title: Thirty-three things every girl should know about women's history. II. Bolden, Tonya.

HQ1410.A133 2002 305.4'0973—dc21 2001047131

Printed in the United States of America

14 13 12 11 10 9

For Nancy Hinkel,
who makes such wise use of the so-much (!) that she knows,
and who so marvelously keeps the "Onward!" going.

CONTENTS

33 Things Every Girl Should Know About Women's History is hardly the whole story. It is a point of entry, a beginning, to the true (and quite intense) tale of women's woes and women's winnings in America, from the eighteenth through the twentieth century.

There is poetry and fiction. There is art and essay (a nice helping of photographs as well). There is grace, courage, pain, outrage, drama (literally): not a little heat and so much light about the suffrage movement, the Equal Rights Amendment, unforgettable firsts, magazines and money, fashion and feminism, and much more, from a Coline and a Joline . . . a Judy . . . two Anns . . . an Anastasia and a Shana . . . a Betsy and an Elisabeth and an Elizabeth . . . Magee and Marsha, Norma, Natasha, and Norma . . . Safiya and Suheir . . . Sue and E. Susan and Fran and Fritz . . . Patricia and Paula . . . Roberta and Rosalie, two Kathleens, Ilene, Ophira, and other vital voices. All together a welcome table: a safe, loving place for you to grow your minds (more), open your eyes (wider), understand and recognize the who, what, when, where, how—and the why—of the more equitable, richer lives of twenty-first-century females compared to that of girls and women long ago.

Compiling *33 Things Every Girl Should Know About Women's History* was an enlightening experience. I happily admit that I learned more than a thing or two in the process: some things I'd never known and other things, once fuzzy, are now crystal-clear.

More than enlightening, it was an inspiring experience. You see, none of the women who contributed an original piece to this anthology needed another thing to do. They are all busy women, productive women, taking care . . . and taking care—of their families, their careers, their hobbies, themselves.

Yet they answered the call, becoming something of an ad hoc collective, because they believe so sincerely and know so acutely how important it is for every girl in America to know whence she has come. Understanding that women's history is rarely taught as a stand-alone subject in school, they wanted to do their part. And they all are (as am I) hoping that you will do your part with your new (or renewed) knowledge gleaned from this book. That is, share it, pass it on: to your girlfriends, mothers, grandmothers, and aunts; to your brothers and fathers, and to your best boys, too.

—TONYA BOLDEN

1776—The Declaration of Independence Up-to-date—1917

NATIONAL WOMAN SUFFRAGE PUBLISHING CO., Inc.
171 MADISON AVENUE   NEW YORK

by Elizabeth Johnson

Past Is Prologue

When the earth was created

your ancestors gave respect to their ancestors.

They knew where they came from,

but do you?

You can't really call yourself a girl

without knowing what it really means to be a girl.

Being a girl is having the strength and wisdom of

Mary McLeod Bethune, Elizabeth Cady Stanton, and Rita Moreno.

You're feminine-less

for knowing less than you should about

Jane Addams, Sojourner Truth, Eleanor Roosevelt, Betty Friedan, and Wilma

Mankiller.

You should know that Anna Mae Aquash was martyred

for fighting for the rights

she knew her people deserved.

And that Ming-Na has helped create a diverse Hollywood.

And every published woman should know that

Phillis Wheatley was one of the first published women in the United States,

and her words inspired George Washington.

Oh, you know who Mr. Washington is.

But the women who paved the way for you to be

a doctor,

a lawyer,

a writer,

an actress,

or a journalist aren't a part of your everyday story.

That's because you don't see the relevance of Gloria Steinem marching through

America

for woman's rights,

you just see that you have rights.

And you don't know why Dorothy Dandridge changed the movies, or

why Marilyn Monroe was so beautiful.

But you do know that JFK was a president loved by many,

and that Lincoln was assassinated.

You know the exact date Pearl Harbor was bombed.

But you don't know the battles your mother,

grandmother, and great-grandmother waged so you could live a better life.

You can't go anywhere in this world

really

without knowing where you as a woman have been.

To all the feminine-lesses of the 21st century—

With every HisStory is HerStory,

find yours out before it's too late.

"Revolutionary Petunias"

Bloomed in Early America

by Abigail Adams

At the onset of the Revolutionary War in 1775, many patriots believed that the new nation in the making would become a land of liberty for all. Like many Africans (enslaved and free), many women were very disappointed that this turned out not to be.

Abigail Adams was in this number. In her now famous "Remember the Ladies" letter, she urged her husband, John Adams, to do the right thing by women. When Abigail wrote this letter, she was in Braintree, Massachusetts, taking care of hearth and home. John was in Philadelphia, where he, Benjamin Franklin, Thomas Jefferson, and other members of the Continental Congress were soon to draft the Declaration of Independence.

March 31, 1776

. . . . I long to hear that you have declared an independancy—and by the way in the new Code of Laws which I suppose it will be necessary for you to make I desire you would Remember the Ladies, and be more generous and favourable to them than your ancestors. Do not put such unlimited power into the hands of the Husbands. Remember all Men would be tyrants if they could. If perticuliar care and attention is not paid to the Ladies we are determined to foment a Rebelion, and will not hold ourselves bound by any Laws in which we have no voice, or Representation.

That your Sex are Naturally Tyrannical is a Truth so thoroughly established as to admit of no dispute, but such of you as wish to be happy willingly give up the harsh title of Master for the more tender and endearing one of Friend. Why then, not put it out of the power of the vicious and the Lawless to use us with cruelty and indignity with impunity. Men of Sense in all Ages abhor those customs which treat us only as the vassals of your Sex. Regard us then as Beings placed by providence under your protection and in immitation of the Supreem Being make use of that power only for our happiness.

John didn't take Abigail's concerns very seriously, as evidenced in his reply, which captures how the majority of people in the United States (including many women) would think about women's rights for a very long time. . . .

April 14, 1776

As to your extraordinary Code of Laws, I cannot but laugh. We have been told that our Struggle has loosened the bands of Government every where. That Children and Apprentices were disobedient—that schools and Colledges were grown turbulent—that Indians slighted their Guardians and Negroes grew insolent to their Masters. But your Letter was the first Intimation that another Tribe more numerous and powerfull than all the rest were grown discontented. —This is rather too coarse a Compliment but you are so saucy, I wont blot it out.

Depend upon it, We know better than to repeal our Masculine systems. Altho they are in full Force, you know they are little more than Theory. We dare not exert our Power in its full Latitude. We are obliged to go fair, and softly, and in Practice you know We are the subjects. We have only the Name of Masters, and rather than give up this, which would compleatly subject Us to the Despotism of the Peticoat, I hope General Washington, and all our brave Heroes would fight. . . .

Abigail's response, dated May 7, 1776, began:

I cannot say that I think you are very generous to the Ladies. . . .

THE WO

by Coline Jenkins-Sahlin

Take a moment and answer these questions—pretend that you are an elected official and asked to vote on the following items. Would you answer yes or no?

A WOMAN SHOULD BE ALLOWED TO . . .

ATTEND COLLEGE   YES   NO

BECOME A LAWYER   YES   NO

PRACTICE MEDICINE   YES   NO

SERVE AS A CHURCH MINISTER   YES   NO

VOTE   YES   NO

HOLD ELECTIVE OFFICE (PRESIDENT, SENATOR, ETC.)   YES   NO

A MARRIED WOMAN SHOULD BE ALLOWED TO . . .

OWN A HOUSE IN HER OWN NAME   YES   NO

SIGN A CONTRACT   YES   NO

OWN THE WAGES SHE EARNS BY WORKING   YES   NO

OWN THE MONEY IN HER OWN BANK ACCOUNT   YES   NO

MEN'S
DECLARATION

Did you answer yes to all the questions? If you did, you agree with the beliefs activist Elizabeth Cady Stanton professed in 1848.

If you answered no, you think like the men who shaped and controlled society, government, church, laws, and the economy of the United States during the mid-nineteenth century. All of these no's created a grossly unfair situation for all women and made them second-class citizens.

Elizabeth Cady Stanton was very frustrated and annoyed by these circumstances. Growing up the daughter of a conservative judge—"a conservative of the conservatives," as she once called him—she was shown that her status as a woman kept her from experiencing the freedoms, educational opportunities, and other benefits that young men of the time were enjoying. When each of her four brothers died tragically young, she attempted to become like the son her father so desperately wanted. She took on the massive task of learning Greek and mastering horseback riding, but no matter how successful her efforts were, her father could only exclaim, "Ah, you should have been a boy."

In 1840, Elizabeth married Henry B. Stanton, an anti-slavery lecturer. Their honeymoon was spent in London, at the World Anti-Slavery Convention. There, she was introduced to a woman who would inspire her with her courage and her friendship throughout their lives—Lucretia Mott. A Quaker minister and mother of five, Lucretia brought Elizabeth into a world of women who discussed the rights of all people with great conviction and determination and made Elizabeth exclaim that "she seemed to understand, as no other woman did, the wrongs, the rights, the capabilities, and the aspirations of all womankind." This dynamic duo would start to change the world for women in years to come.

In 1848, at the home of Jane and Richard Hunt, a tea was held by Quaker women who were interested in a variety of politically radical topics. Lucretia

Mott had asked Mrs. Hunt to invite Elizabeth Cady Stanton. At this gathering, Elizabeth poured out her long-accumulated discontent about the status of women with such vehemence and indignation that she stirred herself—as well as the rest at the meeting—to do and dare anything. "I could not see what to do or where to begin," she later wrote, "my only [hope] was a public meeting for protest and discussion."

The women put down their china cups and listened as the impassioned woman openly admitted to the frustrations of her domestic life and her desire to make the world a more amenable place for all women. These well-bred white ladies, dressed in the simple gray dresses of the Quakers, felt Elizabeth's pain. They, too, were indignant and took on a renewed sense of purpose as Elizabeth challenged them to work together to find a new way to approach these problems.

They determined that Lucretia Mott, well known as a lecturer, would be the perfect draw were they to organize a women's rights convention where these issues could be openly discussed and argued. Before the twilight deepened into night, they resolved to call a convention and wrote out a notice to announce it:

A CONVENTION TO DISCUSS THE SOCIAL, CIVIL, AND RELIGIOUS CONDITION AND RIGHTS OF WOMAN,

WILL BE HELD IN THE WESLEYAN CHAPEL, AT SENECA FALLS, N.Y.,

ON WEDNESDAY AND THURSDAY, THE 19TH AND 20TH OF JULY [1848],

COMMENCING AT 10 O'CLOCK A.M.

The notice was placed in the Seneca County *Courier* on July 11. A few days later, the Ovid (New York) *Bee* and the Rochester *North Star* carried the notice. Elizabeth sent a note to her friend and colleague Elizabeth W. McClintock about preparations for the convention: ——————————————

On July 16, at another tea party, at the home of Mary Ann McClintock in Waterloo, New York, Elizabeth and her friend Mary Ann (as well as the McClintocks' two oldest daughters) set about discussing strategies for change that could be announced to the convention. At this party, tea was

Rain or shine I intend to spend Sunday with you that we may all together concoct a declaration. I have drawn up one but you may suggest any alterations & improvements for I know it is not as perfect a declaration as should go forth from the first woman's rights convention that has ever assembled. I shall take the ten o'clock train in the morning & return at five in the evening, provided we can accomplish all our business in that time. I have written to Lydia Maria Child, Maria Chapman & Sarah Grimké, as we hope for some good letters to read in the convention.

Your friend,
Elizabeth C. Stanton [1]

1 *The Selected Papers of Elizabeth Cady Stanton and Susan B. Anthony.* Vol. I, *In the School of Anti-Slavery, 1840–1866,* ed. Ann D. Gordon (New Brunswick, N.J.: Rutgers University Press, 1997).

merely a beverage, and the issues were put upon the table in place of tea cakes. The issues were clear, but the women wrestled with the form in which to present them. Their frustration was broken when they came upon using the Declaration of Independence as a model for their ideas. What was created at that table that day was the first draft of the Declaration of Sentiments, a listing of the women's concerns. Instead of "King George" as the egregious royalty against which the patriots declared independence in 1776, the women inserted the words "all men." Their hard-hitting document was to be readied for reading to the convention crowd on July 19.

The Declaration of Sentiments contained the following words in its opening:

WE HOLD THESE TRUTHS TO BE SELF-EVIDENT: THAT ALL MEN AND WOMEN ARE CREATED EQUAL; THAT THEY ARE ENDOWED BY THEIR CREATOR WITH CERTAIN INALIENABLE RIGHTS; THAT AMONG THESE ARE LIFE, LIBERTY AND THE PURSUIT OF HAPPINESS.

Just as in 1776, when the men of America wrote a list of grievances against the King of England and his autocratic rule, so did Elizabeth and her friends list their grievances about the autocratic rule of men over women in America, with the following very bold sentiments in the Declaration's fourth paragraph:

THE HISTORY OF MANKIND IS A HISTORY OF REPEATED INJURIES AND USURPATIONS ON THE PART OF MAN TOWARD WOMAN, HAVING IN DIRECT OBJECT THE ESTABLISHMENT OF AN ABSOLUTE TYRANNY OVER HER. TO PROVE THIS, LET THE FACTS BE SUBMITTED TO A CANDID WORLD.

These facts included:

- HE HAS COMPELLED HER TO SUBMIT TO LAW IN THE FORMATION OF WHICH SHE HAD NO VOICE.

- HE HAS MADE HER, IF MARRIED, IN THE EYE OF THE LAW, CIVILLY DEAD.

- HE HAS TAKEN FROM HER ALL RIGHT IN PROPERTY, EVEN TO THE WAGES SHE EARNS.

- . . . IN THE COVENANT OF MARRIAGE, SHE IS COMPELLED TO PROMISE OBEDIENCE TO HER HUSBAND, HE BECOMING, TO ALL INTENTS AND PURPOSES, HER MASTER—THE LAW GIVING HIM POWER TO DEPRIVE HER OF HER LIBERTY AND TO ADMINISTER CHASTISEMENT.

- HE HAS MONOPOLIZED NEARLY ALL THE PROFITABLE EMPLOYMENTS, AND FROM THOSE SHE IS PERMITTED TO FOLLOW, SHE RECEIVES BUT A SCANTY REMUNERATION. HE CLOSES AGAINST HER ALL THE AVENUES OF WEALTH AND DISTINCTION WHICH HE CONSIDERS MOST HONORABLE TO HIMSELF. AS TEACHER OF THEOLOGY, MEDICINE, OR LAW SHE IS NOT KNOWN.

- HE HAS DENIED HER THE FACILITIES FOR OBTAINING A THOROUGH EDUCATION, ALL COLLEGES BEING CLOSED AGAINST HER.

- HE ALLOWS HER IN CHURCH, AS WELL AS STATE, BUT A SUB-ORDINATE POSITION. . . .

Topping the list of facts was this:

- HE HAS NEVER PERMITTED HER TO EXERCISE HER INALIENABLE RIGHT TO THE ELECTIVE FRANCHISE.

This matter of elective franchise, more commonly known as the vote, was the thorniest issue.

"Thou will make us look ridiculous!" exclaimed Lucretia Mott. Like others in the group, Lucretia feared that demanding voting rights for women would jeopardize all their other, more modest requests.

"Women must have the vote," Elizabeth countered. "It is the right by which all other rights are secured." Finally, the women agreed to adopt the demand for the vote. They were going for broke.

NOW, IN VIEW OF THIS ENTIRE DISFRANCHISEMENT OF ONE HALF THE PEOPLE OF THIS COUNTRY, THEIR SOCIAL AND RELIGIOUS DEGRADATION, IN VIEW OF THE UNJUST LAWS ABOVE MENTIONED, AND BECAUSE WOMEN DO FEEL THEMSELVES AGGRIEVED, OPPRESSED, AND FRAUDULENTLY DEPRIVED OF THEIR MOST SACRED RIGHTS, WE INSIST THAT THEY HAVE IMMEDIATE ADMISSION TO ALL THE RIGHTS AND PRIVILEGES WHICH BELONG TO THEM AS CITIZENS OF THE UNITED STATES.

The women did not expect their concerns and demands to be met without a fight nor without great expenditure of energy on their part. The Declaration's final paragraph acknowledged as much:

IN ENTERING UPON THE GREAT WORK BEFORE US, WE ANTICIPATE NO SMALL AMOUNT OF MISCONCEPTION, MISREPRESENTATION, AND RIDICULE; BUT WE SHALL USE EVERY INSTRUMENTALITY WITHIN OUR POWER TO EFFECT OUR OBJECT. WE SHALL EMPLOY AGENTS, CIRCULATE TRACTS, PETITION THE STATE AND NATIONAL LEGISLATURES, AND ENDEAVOR TO ENLIST THE PULPIT AND THE PRESS IN OUR BEHALF. . . .

There followed twelve resolutions, which identified each of the rights that the writers hoped the Declaration would help to acquire for all women. They included the right to vote, the right to hold office, the right to be equal in all ways to men, intellectually, religiously, socially, politically.

This eloquent sixteen-hundred-word document was made complete and ready to be presented to the world on the first day of the convention, Wednesday, July 19, 1848. In less than ten days, a handful of women had conceived and organized America's first women's rights convention.

On that Wednesday, the day of the convention, disaster struck: the church doors were locked. Nobody had the key, so they hoisted Elizabeth's son through an open window to unlock the door. To their amazement, more than three hundred people gathered for this two-day convention. None of the attendees were famous, except for Lucretia Mott and her husband, and Frederick Douglass. Most of them were from the small local communities in upstate New York. They included a glove maker, farmers, professionals, a shopkeeper, mothers and daughters, husbands and wives, aunts and cousins. The youngest was fourteen years old; the oldest, sixty-eight.

With fire in her belly, Elizabeth Cady Stanton stood at a podium, faced the excited crowd with the hope of riling them to passionate depths with her reading of what was by then titled the Declaration of Rights and Sentiments. She felt strongly about what she was about to read and yet, without the benefit of years of public speaking, she was a little nervous.

Finding her voice after a moment, she spoke forcefully about the issues she felt would empower American women. The Declaration and its resolutions were found favorable to the sixty women who signed it as well as the other members of the "promiscuous" (or, mixed sex) crowd—namely, thirty-two men who were "present in favor of the movement."

As word of the convention was released to the press, there arose naysayers—mostly men—who began speaking out against this women's Declaration, in all available media and in public arenas, such as pulpits and legislatures. Not all men were in opposition to the Declaration. Frederick Douglass, a prominent anti-slavery leader of the day, supported their cause and wrote in their defense in the *North Star*. "Indeed," said Douglass, "a discussion of the rights of animals would be regarded with far more complacency by many of what are called the wise and the good of our land than would be a discussion of the rights of women." Douglass hailed the convention as "the most momentous reform that had yet been launched on the world."

No matter who supported or opposed it, the women's rights revolution was on. "Men, their rights, and nothing more; women, their rights, and nothing less." That was the battle cry. And it rose high and strong amidst the growing number of women who would take to the streets and risk their lives and reputations to ensure that their rights as citizens of the United States of America would become part of the national Constitution. It would be a long battle ahead, but these were determined women.

For the next century and a half, the women's movement marched on to many different victories. Some would come sooner than others—for example, in Mississippi in 1839, women were given the right to own property separate from their husbands. However, it took until 1920 for women to get the right to vote nationwide. All the while the Declaration of Rights and Sentiments stood behind the champions of women's rights—inspiring and reenergizing them.

To date, no one knows what happened to the original document. (Perhaps it is a treasure hidden in someone's attic.) Regardless, the Declaration remains the blueprint for one of the most proactive social movements in this country's history. Because of it, our nation is so much stronger. And my backbone is strengthened when I compare my life with that of Elizabeth Cady Stanton, my great-great-grandmother. More than 150 years ago, she could NOT go to college, vote, hold a governmental office, or own property as a married woman, whereas I have gone to college, earned a master's degree, and voted in every election. I serve as a legislator in my town government. I own real estate and have bank accounts in my name. I am a television producer of programs that empower women, and I serve on the board of a museum whose mission is to tell about women's contributions to America. I know I stand on the shoulders of the women and men who went before me fighting for my rights. I stand taller because of them.

Will you?

YES NO

Girls Were Once Happy for Homework

by M. Carey Thomas

Martha Carey Thomas, born on January 2, 1857, was a member of a well-to-do Quaker family in Baltimore, Maryland. As the following excerpts from her teenage diary reveal, this girl (who hated her first name and was known as "Min" or "Minnie" as a child) was passionate about getting a quality education at a time when relatively few women attended college.

January 1, 1871

Well!! I am determined to keep up *this* Journal even though my last attempt was *not* successful and in order to begin right I have commenced on the first day of the new year.

Now my resolutions. . . . I ain't going to be afraid of saying what I think as my journal ain't going to "peach" and I am going to do my best to seclude it from the public gaze.

Here goes for the resolutions. I am going to study my lessons a great deal harder, especially Latin and Greek. I am going to bend my energies to get a good knowledge of Chemistry even though I *do* have to study it by myself. I am going to try not to read many novels as I really think it a waste of time and I *do* want to be a *real* Christian and not a half a one and really let my light *"shine"*. . . .

February 26, 1871

I have at length come to the conclusion that it will be more interesting to me when as an old dried up woman with aid of spectacles I decipher these scrawls to read what I thought than what I did and accordingly I am going to commit my reflections to paper trusting to kind fortune to keep them from careless eyes.

An English man Joseph Beck was here to dinner the other day and he don't believe in the Education of Women. Neither does Cousin Frank King and my such a disgusson as they had. Mother of course was for. They said that they didn't see any good of a womans learning Latin or Greek it didn't make them any more entertaining to their *husbands*. A woman had plenty of other things to do sewing, cooking, taking care of children dressing and flirting. . . . In fact they talked as if the whole end and aim of a woman's life was to get *married* and when she attained that *greatest state of earthly bliss* it was her duty to amuse her husband and to learn nothing; never to exercise the powers of her mind so that he might have the *exquisite* pleasure of knowing more than his wife. Of course they talked the usual cant of woman being too *high* too *exalted* to do anything but sit up in perfect ignorance with folded hands and let men worship at her shrine, meaning in other words like all the rest of such high faluting stuff that woman ought to be *mere dolls* for men to be amused with, to kiss, fondle, pet and love maybe, but as for associating with them on terms of equality they wouldn't think of such a thing. Now I don't mean to say these two men believed this but these were the principles they upheld. I got perfectly enraged. How *unjust*—how narrow-minded—how *utterly uncomprehensible* to deny that women ought to be educated and worse than all to deny that they have equal powers of mind. If I ever live and grow up my *one* aim and consentrated purpose *shall* be and is to show that a woman *can learn can reason can compete* with men in the grand fields of literature and science and conjecture that opens before the 19 century; that a woman can be a woman and a *true* one, with out having all her time engrossed by dress and society. . . .

January 1, 1872

This is the first day of the new year. . . .

What I want almost more than anything else in the world is to go to Vassar. When I go to bed I think about it, and when I get up I think about it. Mama has almost promised to let me go when I'm 17, so that this time two years I would be there. My plan is to try for the sophomore class if possible because if I didn't, the four years there and three years in Philadelphia [at medical school] will make seven years away from home. But the trouble is I'm afraid I can't enter the Sophomore for I have to be examined in Algebra and Geometry besides lots of Greek. The truth is I don't study hard enough . . . I *will* and *must* . . . I do want a good education so much and I've got as good sense as most people and *can* learn if I get a chance and therefore what's to prevent it? Only my laziness—*Bah.*[2]

January 20, 1872

I have just come from a lecture on "Soul and Body" by Thomas Guard, and though it is 10:30 and I have a composition to write this evening I must tell something about it. . . .

In the course of his lecture he said that men's brains in comparison with their size weighed more than any other animal. That the whale's with his immense size only weighed 80 oz. and man's almost 50, but he said one very insulking thing, that *ladies' brains weighed a few ozs less than men's.* He said, "But let them ask *us* for counsel, here are our brains! Let them ask *us* for love, here are our hearts! Let them ask us for worshipers,

---

2 At this point she was attending the Howland Institute, a Quaker all-girl boarding school in upstate New York. At the time, women who wanted to go to college had few choices: of the nearly 600 colleges in America at the time, there were about 70 that were for women and only about 170 that were coeducational. Thomas would eventually decide against attending Vassar or any other all-women's college, in her pursuit of a high-caliber education.

here are our knees!" And the stupid audience applauded him. . . . But if our brains did weigh less, what does it show? Why that for hundreds and thousands of years women haven't had the same education as men, that they have not had the same chances for developing, that with all their force and power men have been keeping them down and forcing them to remain in the narrow sphere of *household* duties and anything beyond that was in the highest degree "undecorous, unrefined, coarse, UNladylike." What a burning shame! And then they sit down and laugh and say "Don't talk any more to *us* of *your* equal powers of intellect, *your* very brains weigh less. The thing is ridiculous!" IDIOTS! Why if woman's brains *did* weigh as much with the infinitely inferior education they receive, what would they weigh when cultivated to the extent men's are? Well! One thing I am determined on, and that is that by the time I die *my* brain shall weigh as much as an *man's* if study and learning can make it so. Then I'll leave it in the hands of some physiologist to be weighed so as after that no miserable man can stand up on a miserable platform and tell [that it is] a "FEW (that is eight ounces)" less than any other man's.

Just wait till equal education takes place and see if that remark can be made!!!!!!!!!!

July 16, 1875

Well, it is *done:* on the 13, 14, 15 of last June I passed the entrance examinations at Cornell University for the Admission into the Classical Course. This last summer it seemed impossible. But the whole of this year with a steady, unalterable determination that surprised myself even—I have been working for it. Father was terribly opposed. . . . Again and again last winter did the old difficulty of deciding between "duty to ourselves and others" come up—for it was not a religious duty of course to go to Cornell and sometimes it seemed as it ought to be given up. . . . Then too the difficulty of preparing without knowing how they examined. . . .

I never did such terrible studying every moment for those three weeks. . . . However, it is over with—Professor Peck said I passed a splendid examination in Latin, ditto Professor Oliver in Algebra and Geometry. . . . Almost all the professors complimented Father and Mother upon my passing so well. Mr.

Howland when he saw me said he was proud that a *Howland* graduate, etc., etc. The strain was terrible because I could not have endured failure. And it was an inexpressible satisfaction to pass well. Father and Mother were up there and explored the university while I was getting examined. Mother was delighted with it and I think Father was pleased. The last night he said to me, "Well Minnie, I'm proud of thee, but this university is an awful place to swallow thee up."

If I can help it he and Mother shall never regret having yielded to me in this thing.

Thomas entered Cornell as a junior and graduated in 1877 with a B.A. After a frustrating year at Johns Hopkins University (where she was not permitted to study in classes with men), Thomas studied abroad: first at the University of Leipzig (where in classes she had to sit behind a screen so as not be a distraction to her male classmates and which did not grant women Ph.D.'s) and then at the University of Zurich, where in 1882 she received a Ph.D. summa cum laude, the first woman and the first foreigner to do so. After a year of study at the Sorbonne, Thomas returned to America, where she soon embarked upon what would be an illustrious career as an educator at a newly established Quaker women's college outside Philadelphia, Bryn Mawr. Unfortunately, this fierce advocate of the development of women's minds was not committed to the development of all people's minds. Thomas was a supporter of the eugenics movement of the early 20th century, which used bogus science to propagate the notion of the innate intellectual supremacy of northern Europeans. In her address at Bryn Mawr's opening convocation of 1916, Thomas exalted that the student body was "overwhelmingly English, Scotch, Irish, Welsh and other admixtures of French, German, Dutch largely predominant. All other strains are negligible. . . ." She went on to add, "You, the students of Bryn Mawr, have the best intellectual inheritance the world affords." [3]

---

3 Quoted in *The Making of a Feminist: Early Journals and Letters of M. Carey Thomas,* ed. Marjorie Housepian Dobkin (Kent, Oh.: Kent State University Press, 1979).

5

by Charlotte Perkins Gilman

"THE YELLOW WALLPAPER"

"It was not intended to drive people crazy, but to save people from being driven crazy, and it worked." This, from Charlotte Perkins Gilman's essay "Why I Wrote 'The Yellow Wallpaper'" (The Forerunner, 1912), in which Gilman revealed how autobiographical her now classic short story was. "The Yellow Wallpaper," first published in The New England Magazine in 1892, did indeed make some people "crazy": those who were threatened at how well Gilman captured an "affliction" many well-to-do women suffered during the Gilded Age: being stifled, being imprisoned by the idea that to exercise the life of their minds would do them irrevocable harm. Some women accepted the status quo, and abided by the established pattern of life set forth by the "cult of domesticity." Others broke free, often becoming "outcasts" of their social class. Still others lapsed into depression (or worse) under the weight of how silly and dependent a "proper" woman was supposed to be—the fate of the protagonist of Gilman's "The Yellow Wallpaper," an abridged version of which follows.

It is very seldom that mere ordinary people like John and myself secure ancestral halls for the summer.

A colonial mansion, a hereditary estate, I would say a haunted house and reach the height of romantic felicity—but that would be asking too much of fate!

Still I will proudly declare that there is something queer about it.

Else, why should it be let so cheaply? And why have stood so long untenanted?

John laughs at me, of course, but one expects that.

John is practical in the extreme. He has no patience with faith, an intense horror of superstition, and he scoffs openly at any talk of things not to be felt and seen and put down in figures.

John is a physician, and *perhaps*—(I would not say it to a living soul, of course, but this is dead paper and a great relief to my mind)—*perhaps* that is one reason I do not get well faster.

You see, he does not believe I am sick! And what can one do?

If a physician of high standing, and one's own husband, assures friends and relatives that there is really nothing the matter with one but temporary nervous depression—a slight hysterical tendency—what is one to do?

My brother is also a physician, and also of high standing, and he says the same thing.

So I take phosphates or phosphites—whichever it is—and tonics, and air and exercise, journeys, and am absolutely forbidden to "work" until I am well again.

Personally, I disagree with their ideas.

Personally, I believe that congenial work, with excitement and change, would do me good.

But what is one to do?

I did write for a while in spite of them; but it *does* exhaust me a good deal—having to be so sly about it, or else meet with heavy opposition.

I sometimes fancy that in my condition, if I had less opposition and more society and stimulus—but John says the very worst thing I can do is to think about my condition, and I confess it always makes me feel bad.

So I will let it alone and talk about the house.

The most beautiful place! It is quite alone, standing well back from the road, quite three miles from the village. It makes me think of English places that you read about, for there are hedges and walls and gates that lock, and lots of separate little houses for the gardeners and people.

There is a *delicious* garden! I never saw such a garden—large and shady, full of box-bordered paths, and lined with long grape-covered arbors with seats under them.

There were greenhouses, but they are all broken now.

There was some legal trouble, I believe, something about the heirs and co-heirs; anyhow, the place has been empty for years.

That spoils my ghostliness, I am afraid, but I don't care—there is something strange about the house—I can feel it.

I even said so to John one moonlight evening, but he said what I felt was a draught, and shut the window.

I get unreasonably angry with John sometimes. I'm sure I never used to be so sensitive. I think it is due to this nervous condition.

But John says if I feel so I shall neglect proper self-control; so I take pains to control myself—before him, at least, and that makes me very tired.

I don't like our room a bit. I wanted one downstairs that opened onto the piazza and had roses all over the window, and such pretty old-fashioned chintz hangings! But John would not hear of it.

He said there was only one window and not room for two beds, and no near room for him if he took another.

He is very careful and loving, and hardly lets me stir without special direction.

I have a schedule prescription for each hour in the day; he takes all care from me, and so I feel basely ungrateful not to value it more.

He said he came here solely on my account, that I was to have perfect rest and all the air I could get. "Your exercise depends on your strength, my dear," said he, "and your food somewhat on your appetite; but air you can absorb all the time." So we took the nursery at the top of the house.

It is a big, airy room, the whole floor nearly, with windows that look all ways, and air and sunshine galore. It was nursery first, and then playroom and gymnasium, I should judge, for the windows are barred for little children, and there are rings and things in the walls.

The paint and paper look as if a boys' school had used it. It is stripped off—the paper—in great patches all around the head of my bed, about as far as I can reach, and in a great place on the other side of the room low down. I never saw a worse paper in my life. One of those sprawling, flamboyant patterns committing every artistic sin.

It is dull enough to confuse the eye in following, pronounced enough constantly to irritate and provoke study, and when you follow the lame uncertain curves for a little distance they suddenly commit suicide—plunge off at outrageous angles, destroy themselves in unheard-of contradictions.

The color is repellent, almost revolting: a smouldering unclean yellow, strangely faded by the slow-turning sunlight. It is a dull yet lurid orange in some places, a sickly sulphur tint in others.

No wonder the children hated it! I should hate it myself if I had to live in this room long.

There comes John, and I must put this away—he hates to have me write a word.

• • •

We have been here two weeks, and I haven't felt like writing before, since that first day.

I am sitting by the window now, up in this atrocious nursery, and there is nothing to hinder my writing as much as I please, save lack of strength. . . .

It is fortunate Mary is so good with the baby. Such a dear baby!

And yet I *cannot* be with him, it makes me so nervous. . . .

I'm really getting quite fond of the big room, all but that horrid paper.

Out of one window I can see the garden—those mysterious deep-shaded arbors, the riotous old-fashioned flowers, and bushes and gnarly trees.

Out of another I get a lovely view of the bay and a little private wharf belonging to the estate. There is a beautiful shaded lane that runs down there from the house. I always fancy I see people walking in these numerous paths and arbors, but John has cautioned me not to give way to fancy in the least. He says that with my imaginative power and habit of story-making, a nervous weakness like mine is sure to lead to all manner of excited fancies, and that I ought to use my will and good sense to check the tendency. So I try.

I think sometimes that if I were only well enough to write a little it would relieve the press of ideas and rest me.

But I find I get pretty tired when I try.

It is so discouraging not to have any advice and companionship about my work. When I get really well, John says we will ask Cousin Henry and Julia down for a long visit; but he says he would as soon put fireworks in my pillow-case as to let me have those stimulating people about now.

I wish I could get well faster.

But I must not think about that. This paper looks to me as if it *knew* what a vicious influence it had!

There is a recurrent spot where the pattern lolls like a broken neck and two bulbous eyes stare at you upside down.

I get positively angry with the impertinence of it and the everlasting-ness. Up and down and sideways they crawl, and those absurd unblinking eyes are everywhere. There is one place where two breadths didn't match, and the eyes go all up and down the line, one a little higher than the other.

I never saw so much expression in an inanimate thing before, and we all know how much expression they have! I used to lie awake as a child and get more entertainment and terror out of blank walls and plain furniture than most children could find in a toy-store.

I remember what a kindly wink the knobs of our big old bureau used to have, and there was one chair that always seemed like a strong friend.

I used to feel that if any of the other things looked too fierce I could always hop into that chair and be safe.

The furniture in this room is no worse than inharmonious, however, for we had to bring it all from downstairs. I suppose when this was used as a playroom they had to take the nursery things out, and no wonder! I never saw such ravages as the children have made here.

The wallpaper, as I said before, is torn off in spots, and it sticketh closer than a brother—they must have had perseverance as well as hatred.

Then the floor is scratched and gouged and splintered, the plaster itself is dug out here and there, and this great heavy bed, which is all we found in the room, looks as if it had been through the wars.

But I don't mind it a bit—only the paper.

There comes John's sister. Such a dear girl as she is, and so careful of me! I must not let her find me writing.

She is a perfect and enthusiastic housekeeper, and hopes for no better profession! I verily believe she thinks it is the writing which made me sick!

But I can write when she is out, and see her a long way off from these windows. . . .

This wallpaper has a kind of sub-pattern in a different shade, a particularly irritating one, for you can only see it in certain lights, and not clearly then.

But in the places where it isn't faded and where the sun is just so— I can see a strange, provoking, formless sort of figure, that seems to skulk about behind that silly and conspicuous front design.

There's sister on the stairs!

Well, the Fourth of July is over! The people are all gone, and I am tired out. John thought it might do me good to see a little company, so we just had Mother and Nellie and the children down for a week.

Of course I didn't do a thing. Jennie sees to everything now.

But it tired me all the same.

John says if I don't pick up faster he shall send me to Weir Mitchell in the fall.

But I don't want to go there at all. I had a friend who was in his hands once, and she says he is just like John and my brother, only more so!

Besides, it is such an undertaking to go so far.

I don't feel as if it was worthwhile to turn my hand over for anything, and I'm getting dreadfully fretful and querulous.

I cry at nothing, and cry most of the time.

Of course I don't when John is here, or anybody else, but when I am alone.

And I am alone a good deal just now. John is kept in town very often by serious cases, and Jennie is good and lets me alone when I want her to.

So I walk a little in the garden or down that lovely lane, sit on the porch under the roses, and lie down up here a good deal.

I'm getting really fond of the room in spite of the wallpaper. Perhaps *because* of the wallpaper.

It dwells in my mind so!

I lie here on this great immovable bed—it is nailed down, I believe— and follow that pattern about by the hour. It is as good as gymnastics, I assure you. I start, we'll say, at the bottom, down in the corner over there where it has not been touched, and I determine for the thousandth time that I *will follow* that pointless pattern to some sort of a conclusion.

I know a little of the principle of design, and I know this thing was not arranged on any laws of radiation, or alternation, or repetition, or symmetry, or anything else that I ever heard of.

It is repeated, of course, by the breadths, but not otherwise.

Looked at in one way, each breadth stands alone; the bloated curves and flourishes—a kind of "debased Romanesque" with delirium tremens— go waddling up and down in isolated columns of fatuity.

But, on the other hand, they connect diagonally, and the sprawling outlines run off in great slanting waves of optic horror, like a lot of wallowing sea-weeds in full chase.

The whole thing goes horizontally, too, at least it seems so, and I exhaust myself trying to distinguish the order of its going in that direction.

They have used a horizontal breadth for a frieze, and that adds wonderfully to the confusion.

There is one end of the room where it is almost intact, and there, when the crosslights fade and the low sun shines directly upon it, I can almost fancy radiation after all—the interminable grotesque seems to form around a common center and rush off in headlong plunges of equal distraction.

It makes me tired to follow it. I will take a nap, I guess.

I don't know why I should write this.

I don't want to.

I don't feel able.

And I know John would think it absurd. But I must say what I feel and think in some way—it is such a relief!

But the effort is getting to be greater than the relief.

Half the time now I am awfully lazy, and lie down ever so much. John says I mustn't lose my strength, and has me take cod liver oil and lots of tonics and things, to say nothing of ale and wine and rare meat.

Dear John! He loves me very dearly, and hates to have me sick. I tried to have a real earnest reasonable talk with him the other day, and tell him how I wish he would let me go and make a visit to Cousin Henry and Julia.

But he said I wasn't able to go, nor able to stand it after I got there; and I did not make out a very good case for myself, for I was crying before I had finished.

It is getting to be a great effort for me to think straight. Just this nervous weakness, I suppose.

And dear John gathered me up in his arms, and just carried me upstairs and laid me on the bed, and sat by me and read to me till it tired my head. . . .

There's one comfort—the baby is well and happy, and does not have to occupy this nursery with the horrid wallpaper. . . .

There are things in that wallpaper that nobody knows about but me, or ever will.

Behind that outside pattern the dim shapes get clearer every day.

It is always the same shape, only very numerous.

And it is like a woman stooping down and creeping about behind that pattern. I don't like it a bit. I wonder—I begin to think—I wish John would take me away from here!

It is so hard to talk with John about my case, because he is so wise, and because he loves me so.

But I tried it last night.

It was moonlight. The moon shines in all around just as the sun does.

I hate to see it sometimes, it creeps so slowly, and always comes in by one window or another.

John was asleep and I hated to waken him, so I kept still and watched the moonlight on that undulating wallpaper till I felt creepy.

The faint figure behind seemed to shake the pattern, just as if she wanted to get out.

I got up softly and went to feel and see if the paper *did* move, and when I came back John was awake.

"What is it, little girl?" he said. "Don't go walking about like that—you'll get cold."

I thought it was a good time to talk, so I told him that I really was not gaining here, and that I wished he would take me away.

"Why, darling!" said he. "Our lease will be up in three weeks, and I can't see how to leave before.

"The repairs are not done at home, and I cannot possibly leave town just now. Of course, if you were in any danger, I could and would, but you really are better, dear, whether you can see it or not. I am a doctor, dear, and I know. You are gaining flesh and color, your appetite is better, I feel really much easier about you."

"I don't weigh a bit more," said I, "nor as much; and my appetite may be better in the evening when you are here but it is worse in the morning when you are away!"

"Bless her little heart!" said he with a big hug. "She shall be as sick as she pleases! But now let's improve the shining hours by going to sleep, and talk about it in the morning!". . .

We went to sleep before long. He thought I was asleep first, but I wasn't, and lay there for hours trying to decide whether that front pattern and the back pattern really did move together or separately.

On a pattern like this, by daylight, there is a lack of sequence, a defiance of law, that is a constant irritant to a normal mind.

The color is hideous enough, and unreliable enough, and infuriating enough, but the pattern is torturing.

You think you have mastered it, but just as you get well under way in following, it turns a back-somersault and there you are. It slaps you in the face, knocks you down, and tramples upon you. It is like a bad dream.

The outside pattern is a florid arabesque, reminding one of a fungus. If you can imagine a toadstool in joints, an interminable string of toadstools, budding and sprouting in endless convolutions—why, that is something like it.

That is, sometimes!

There is one marked peculiarity about this paper, a thing nobody seems to notice but myself, and that is that it changes as the light changes.

When the sun shoots in through the east window—I always watch for that first long, straight ray—it changes so quickly that I never can quite believe it.

That is why I watch it always.

By moonlight—the moon shines in all night when there is a moon—I wouldn't know it was the same paper.

At night in any kind of light, in twilight, candlelight, lamplight, and worst of all by moonlight, it becomes bars! The outside pattern, I mean, and the woman behind it is as plain as can be.

I didn't realize for a long time what the thing was that showed behind, that dim sub-pattern, but now I am quite sure it is a woman.

By daylight she is subdued, quiet. I fancy it is the pattern that keeps her so still. It is so puzzling. It keeps me quiet by the hour.

I lie down ever so much now. John says it is good for me, and to sleep all I can.

Indeed he started the habit by making me lie down for an hour after each meal.

It is a very bad habit, I am convinced, for you see, I don't sleep.

And that cultivates deceit, for I don't tell them I'm awake—oh, no!

The fact is I am getting a little afraid of John.

He seems very queer sometimes, and even Jennie has an inexplicable look.

It strikes me occasionally, just as a scientific hypothesis, that perhaps it is the paper!

I have watched John when he did not know I was looking, and come into the room suddenly on the most innocent excuses, and I've caught him several times *looking at the paper*! And Jennie too. I caught Jennie with her hand on it once.

She didn't know I was in the room, and when I asked her in a quiet, a very quiet voice, with the most restrained manner possible, what she was doing with the paper—she turned around as if she had been caught stealing, and looked quite angry—asked me why I should frighten her so!

Then she said that the paper stained everything it touched, that she had found yellow smooches on all my clothes and John's, and she wished we would be more careful!

Did not that sound innocent? But I know she was studying that pattern, and I am determined that nobody shall find it out but myself!

Life is very much more exciting now than it used to be. You see, I have something more to expect, to look forward to, to watch. I really do eat better, and am more quiet than I was.

John is so pleased to see me improve! He laughed a little the other day, and said I seemed to be flourishing in spite of my wallpaper.

I turned it off with a laugh. I had no intention of telling him it was *because* of the wallpaper—he would make fun of me. He might even want to take me away.

I don't want to leave now until I have found it out. There is a week more, and I think that will be enough.

I'm feeling ever so much better!

I don't sleep much at night, for it is so interesting to watch developments; but I sleep a good deal in the daytime.

In the daytime it is tiresome and perplexing.

There are always new shoots on the fungus, and new shades of yellow all over it. I cannot keep count of them, though I have tried conscientiously.

It is the strangest yellow, that wallpaper! It makes me think of all the yellow things I ever saw—not beautiful ones like buttercups, but old, foul, bad yellow things.

But there is something else about that paper—the smell! I noticed it the moment we came into the room, but with so much air and sun it was not bad. Now we have had a week of fog and rain, and whether the windows are open or not, the smell is here.

It creeps all over the house.

I find it hovering in the dining-room, skulking in the parlor, hiding in the hall, lying in wait for me on the stairs.

It gets into my hair.

Even when I go to ride, if I turn my head suddenly and surprise it—there is that smell!

Such a peculiar odor, too! I have spent hours in trying to analyze it, to find what it smelled like.

It is not bad—at first—and very gentle, but quite the subtlest, most enduring odor I ever met.

In this damp weather it is awful. I wake up in the night and find it hanging over me.

It used to disturb me at first. I thought seriously of burning the house—to reach the smell.

But now I am used to it. The only thing I can think of that it is like is the *color* of the paper! A yellow smell.

There is a very funny mark on this wall, low down, near the mopboard. A streak that runs round the room. It goes behind every piece of furniture, except the bed, a long, straight, even *smooch,* as if it had been rubbed over and over.

I wonder how it was done and who did it, and what they did it for. Round and round and round—round and round and round—it makes me dizzy!

I really have discovered something at last.

Through watching so much at night, when it changes so, I have finally found out.

The front pattern *does* move—and no wonder! The woman behind shakes it!

Sometimes I think there are a great many women behind, and sometimes only one, and she crawls around fast, and her crawling shakes it all over.

Then in the very bright spots she keeps still, and in the very shady spots she just takes hold of the bars and shakes them hard.

And she is all the time trying to climb through. But nobody could climb through that pattern—it strangles so; I think that is why it has so many heads.

They get through, and then the pattern strangles them off and turns them upside down, and makes their eyes white!

If those heads were covered or taken off it would not be half so bad.

I think that woman gets out in the daytime!

And I'll tell you why—privately—I've seen her!

I can see her out of every one of my windows!

It is the same woman, I know, for she is always creeping, and most women do not creep by daylight.

I see her in that long shaded lane, creeping up and down. I see her in those dark grape arbors, creeping all around the garden.

I see her on that long road under the trees, creeping along, and when a carriage comes she hides under the blackberry vines.

I don't blame her a bit. It must be very humiliating to be caught creeping by daylight!

I always lock the door when I creep by daylight. I can't do it at night, for I know John would suspect something at once.

And John is so queer now that I don't want to irritate him. I wish he would take another room! Besides, I don't want anybody to get that woman out at night but myself.

I often wonder if I could see her out of all the windows at once.

But, turn as fast as I can, I can only see out of one at one time.

And though I always see her, she *may* be able to creep faster than I can turn! I have watched her sometimes away off in the open country, creeping as fast as a cloud shadow in a wind.

If only that top pattern could be gotten off from the under one! I mean to try it, little by little.

I have found out another funny thing, but I shan't tell it this time! It does not do to trust people too much.

There are only two more days to get this paper off, and I believe John is beginning to notice. I don't like the look in his eyes. . . .

Hurrah! This is the last day, but it is enough. John is to stay in town over night, and won't be out until this evening.

Jennie wanted to sleep with me—the sly thing; but I told her I should undoubtedly rest better for a night all alone.

That was clever, for really I wasn't alone a bit! As soon as it was moonlight and that poor thing began to crawl and shake the pattern, I got up and ran to help her.

I pulled and she shook. I shook and she pulled, and before morning we had peeled off yards of that paper.

A strip about as high as my head and half around the room.

And then when the sun came and that awful pattern began to laugh at me, I declared I would finish it today! . . .

I have locked the door and thrown the key down into the front path.

I don't want to go out, and I don't want to have anybody come in, till John comes.

I want to astonish him.

I've got a rope up here that even Jennie did not find. If that woman does get out, and tries to get away, I can tie her!

But I forgot I could not reach far without anything to stand on!

This bed will *not* move!

I tried to lift and push it until I was lame, and then I got so angry I bit off a little piece at one corner—but it hurt my teeth.

Then I peeled off all the paper I could reach standing on the floor. It sticks horribly and the pattern just enjoys it! All those strangled heads and bulbous eyes and waddling fungus growths just shriek with derision!

I am getting angry enough to do something desperate. To jump out of the window would be admirable exercise, but the bars are too strong even to try.

Besides I wouldn't do it. Of course not. I know well enough that a step like that is improper and might be misconstrued.

I don't like to *look* out of the windows even—there are so many of those creeping women, and they creep so fast.

I wonder if they all come out of that wallpaper as I did?

But I am securely fastened now by my well-hidden rope—you don't get *me* out in the road there!

I suppose I shall have to get back behind the pattern when it comes night, and that is hard!

It is so pleasant to be out in this great room and creep around as I please!

I don't want to go outside. I won't, even if Jennie asks me to.

For outside you have to creep on the ground, and everything is green instead of yellow.

But here I can creep smoothly on the floor, and my shoulder just fits in that long smooch around the wall, so I cannot lose my way.

Why there's John at the door!

It is no use, young man, you can't open it!

How he does call and pound!

Now he's crying to Jennie for an axe.

It would be a shame to break down that beautiful door!

"John, dear!" said I in the gentlest voice, "The key is down by the front steps, under a plantain leaf!"

That silenced him for a few moments.

Then he said, very quietly indeed, "Open the door, my darling!"

"I can't," said I. "The key is down by the front door under a plantain leaf!" And then I said it again, several times, very gently and slowly, and said it so often that he had to go and see, and he got it of course, and came in. He stopped short by the door.

"What is the matter?" he cried. "For God's sake, what are you doing!"

I kept on creeping just the same, but I looked at him over my shoulder.

"I've got out at last," said I, "in spite of you and Jane. And I've pulled off most of the paper, so you can't put me back!"

Now why should that man have fainted? But he did, and right across my path by the wall, so that I had to creep over him every time!

6

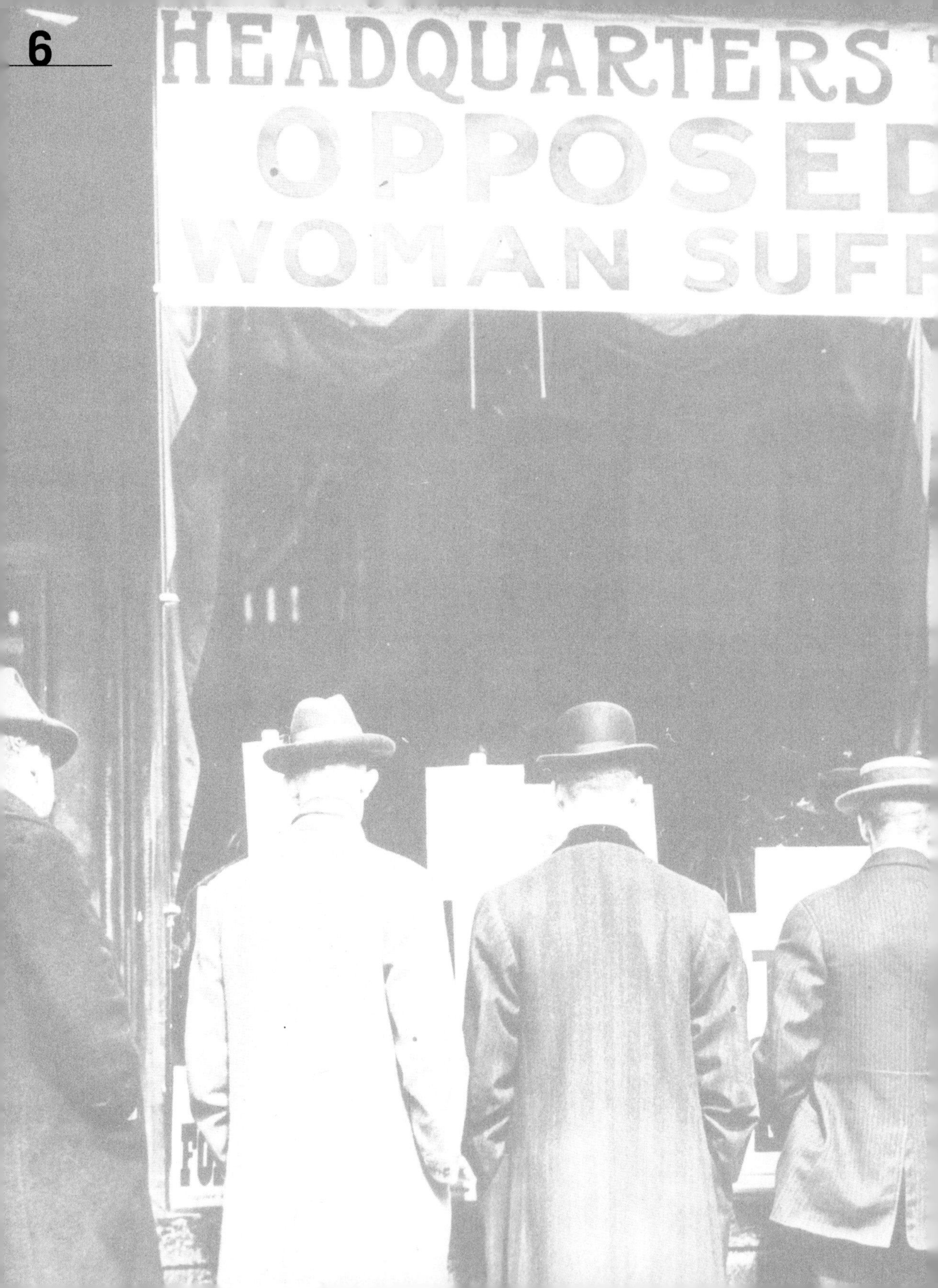

THE WOMEN ONCE VETOED LATER VOTED

by Patricia C. McKissack

On August 18, 1920, the Nineteenth Amendment was ratified, granting women the right to vote. Charlotte Woodward (Woodard) was the only woman who had attended the Seneca Falls convention and signed the Declaration of Sentiments in 1848 and was still alive to exercise her right to vote. When a reporter asked if she planned to go to the polls, she answered sprightly, "I'm going to vote if they have to carry me there on a stretcher!" Woodward voted in the general election, November 2, 1920, and stepped into the pages of history. The following is a fictional monologue—based on historical events, biographies, and interviews—capturing what Woodward, who was, at the time she voted, more than ninety years of age, might have thought when she heard the Nineteenth Amendment had passed.

More than a few reporters have come here to Philadelphia to interview me about my role in the women's suffrage movement. They've been asking about the early leaders. Did I know them? What were they like? What would they think about the ratification of the Nineteenth Amendment? What part did I take in the movement?

To be honest, I'm a bit dismayed by all the commotion. I never sought to be a leader in the voting rights movement, but I'm proud to say I did my part. I admired the gifts of drive and determination that Susan B. Anthony possessed and the eloquence of Elizabeth Cady Stanton. I was always impressed with the quick wit and exuberance of Lucy Stone, the brilliance of Julia Ward Howe, and the tenacity of common sense that Sojourner Truth used so effectively to make fools—or believers—of her critics. And, of course, who could ever maintain the level of courage it took for Frederick Douglass to stand steadfastly with us women when others of his gender turned away. But in my own way I was every bit as committed to the cause as they were—though not at first.

In the winter of 1848, I was a nineteen-year-old, living and working as a glove maker in Waterloo, New York. Being on my own for the first time was considered quite bold. I grew up on a farm with thirteen brothers and sisters— never a moment of privacy, never a time when there wasn't something to do. My father was a hardworking farmer who had raised us to believe that God-fearing, free men were the bedrock of a family's wealth and the source of national prosperity. He had reluctantly allowed me to go to the city to work, with the hopes that I would soon find a husband. As was expected, all my earnings were sent to my father and he allotted me what he felt I should have. At the time, I believed that it was his God-given right to do so, so I never complained.

I missed my big family at first, but I quickly made friends at the boardinghouse where I lived. And of course, I attended church and met other young people my age. I especially grew fond of a young wife and mother named Amelia Lang. We were as different as an apple is from an orange. I was shy and reserved, but she was filled to the brim with boundless enthusiasm and a sense of adventure. Amelia was involved in every cause, from abolition to temperance, and she prodded me into attending a temperance meeting. It didn't take too much persuasion, because I knew firsthand the horrors families suffered due to the abuses of alcohol. I was bound and determined to rid the world of the wicked drink that had done so much to destroy human lives. Besides, I knew my father would approve. So to this end I became firmly committed.

Amelia wanted me to become an active abolitionist, too. The idea excited me at first, but later I declined. Although I was vehemently opposed to slavery, my father felt my energies would best be spent working for one cause rather than spreading myself too thin and accomplishing nothing. Dutifully, I obeyed him. Amelia teased me endlessly about being "the perfectly contented servant."

One early summer day, while attending a temperance meeting, a fellow member addressed us. She had received a letter and handbill from Elizabeth Cady Stanton and Lucretia Mott advertising a Woman's Rights Convention to be held in Seneca Falls, July 19–20, 1848. There was much debate that day among the women at the meeting. And I, for one, wasn't convinced that this was anything that should compel my participation. I remember naively asking Amelia during the walk home, what rights did women need that they didn't already have? Amelia stared at me in amazement; she was too bewildered to answer.

Amelia would not let the subject rest. She used every opportunity to persuade me to attend the Seneca Falls meeting with her. I had only to think what my father would say about such a meeting. When I asked Amelia what her husband thought of her going, she responded matter-of-factly, "My husband takes no interest in my 'meetings' so long as his house is clean, his clothing washed and ironed, his son well behaved, and his supper ready after work. But if he was of a mind to, he could forbid me to go, and if I went anyway, he could beat and imprison me. And it would be completely legal! He could leave me and take our son. All my property belongs to him. Do you think that is right?"

"Well, no . . . ," I answered.

"And do you think it is right that you labor for hours sewing gloves for just a pittance? Yet even those poor wages go to your father. Or when your father or my husband dies the wife and daughters can't inherit a thing? That's slavery."

"I'm not a slave. I'm a young woman."

"There's precious little difference," said Amelia.

I remember spending a sleepless night, thinking about what Amelia had said. Secretly I had entertained the idea that my wages should belong to me, since I had done the work. What had come over me, I thought? Come morning, though, I was convinced that I would go to Seneca Falls and I wasn't going to ask permission either.

With my chores done and with the proper care for Amelia's son provided by a trusted church member, we boarded the wagon with several other women and set out for the convention. It was Wednesday, a clear July morning, and at first we were the only wagon on the road. I wondered if we were going to be the only women bold enough to come. As we reached crossroads, we saw other wagons coming from every part of the county. When we entered the city limits of Seneca Falls, we were part of a long procession. I was never so excited in my whole life.

We made our way to the Wesleyan Chapel past a crowd of curiosity seekers. Once inside, the door was bolted from the inside—no doubt by the parson, who was probably having second thoughts about allowing the church to be used by women to talk about women's issues. It was scandalous, at that time, for a woman to speak in public.

After Amelia and I found seats, I settled my thoughts a bit. I looked around to see who else was in attendance. Thinking back now, it still astonishes me— remembering the sight of so many of my own gender in one place equal to men: no fathers around to scold; no brothers to chide; no husbands to make demands. It was wonderful. There were a handful of men in our midst, including the great orator himself, Frederick Douglass the abolitionist! I had heard him speak before at a meeting I'd attended with Amelia. I'd never forgotten the afternoon we heard him tell about his escape from slavery. Thereafter, he had been a hero of mine.

Save for Douglass there was not another colored person in attendance. Among the three hundred women who came to Seneca Falls, there wasn't one colored woman. I later learned it was not from lack of interest or support that our darker sisters did not join us in the convention, but rather their need to devote every moment to the eradication of slavery. Mr. Douglass, however, spoke with conviction and compassion when he endorsed our concerns and lent his name in support of freedom and legal equality for all people—black, white, rich, poor, men and women. Perhaps, I thought, I will reconsider becoming an abolitionist.

As the day wore on and the oppressive heat took its toll on some of the participants, more than a few ladies had to be spirited away to cooler, less confined spaces. My friend Amelia felt that the very clothing women wore was oppressive. She whispered, "I say that when we loosen the corsets that bind our waists, we will think more freely as well."

As I listened to the powerful messages in the speeches, I felt a passion stirring inside me. I wasn't nearly as shocked by what was being said; I was excited, exhilarated, and my head soaked up new ideas like parched earth in a rainstorm. As Martha Coffin Wright, Jane Hunt, and Mary Ann McClintock talked about the plight of women, I was surprised at how much our situation was similar to what Frederick Douglass had described he'd experienced as a slave. When Amelia had compared women's lives to that of slaves, I'd denied it, but in the truth of love and logic, the facts were unimpeachable. Weren't women indeed treated like chattel? Women were turned away from colleges and discouraged from taking up

a trade. And it was no small thing that women could teach—but only if they were single, and then they made less money than their male counterparts.

Even though decades have passed, I can still hear Elizabeth Cady Stanton reading the Declaration of Sentiments and the twelve resolutions designed to gain equal rights and privileges women of my era were routinely denied. And when they called for delegates to vote on the resolutions relating to equal rights in marriage, education, and employment, Amelia's hand waved like a sheet in the wind. Tentatively, I raised my hand in support, all the time wondering what my brothers would think of me now; what my father would do to me if he knew I was even here, let alone voting for equal protection for women under the law? Soon I was caught up in the excitement of the moment, and I knew that this meeting was the beginning of something much larger than the sum of my whole existence.

Amelia and I were overjoyed when one by one the resolutions passed unanimously. Then came the debate over the resolution that called for the right for women "to secure to themselves their sacred right of franchise." A gathering murmur began rippling through the crowd. Suddenly the mood of the conventioneers changed.

"The right to vote? That's going too far," some of the women argued.

"I want none of this," one woman whispered to another. Some said nothing but left in a huff.

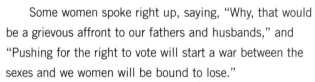

Some women spoke right up, saying, "Why, that would be a grievous affront to our fathers and husbands," and "Pushing for the right to vote will start a war between the sexes and we women will be bound to lose."

The debate between those who were for woman suffrage and those who weren't became strident and mean-spirited. Elizabeth Cady Stanton would not back down; she held her ground and argued persuasively for women's right to vote. Somewhere between the two extremes were women like me who didn't know what to think. In truth, the idea of voting had never occurred to me. But once the words were said, the idea began to take shape in my heart. It would take a while for it to be reconciled in my head.

I listened carefully to the pros and cons and in the end I cast my lot with those who voted for the suffrage resolution and joyfully added my name to it. I was completely surprised, however, when Amelia took the opposite side. Amelia—the one who had pushed and prodded me to take even a small step toward freedom and independence—could not make the leap. "It won't help our cause to be too radical too soon," she said, just as convinced that I was wrong. "I'm afraid such an extreme position will make our cause look foolish." It was my turn to look at her in amazement. Happily, we agreed to disagree and remained friends many years.

Mr. Douglass supported the resolution and urged its passage. And much to his credit, it passed by a very narrow margin and the rest is history. Mr. Douglass hitched a ride back with us in our wagon, and I got a chance to thank him personally for his support. It's not often one gets to thank a legend.

Yes, I left Seneca Falls a changed person. I was filled to capacity with thoughts that I'd never entertained before, but there was a calmness within me—a sense of resolve. I was no longer confused or uncertain. In the course of two days, I—Charlotte Woodward—had become a radical with a whole new perspective on womanhood.

While never reaching the national leadership level of Stanton, Stone, and Anthony, Charlotte Woodward returned to Waterloo and campaigned to change laws that restricted women. Later that same year, New York State passed the Married Woman's Property Act, which allowed women to keep their earnings, invest money, and transact their own business without their husbands' permission; sign contracts, instigate lawsuits, and keep property inherited or received as a gift. By 1860, Indiana, Maine, Missouri, and Ohio had passed similar laws.

Women such as Charlotte Woodward were the backbone of the women's movement. They worked ceaselessly in either the New York–based NWSA, led by Elizabeth Cady Stanton and Susan B. Anthony, or the Boston-based AWSA, led by Lucy Stone and Julia Ward Howe. For two decades these two competing women's organizations held protests, demonstrations, and fought in the courts for equal rights. The greatest achievements were made in the area of women's education and health. And some state constitutions, such as Wyoming's, gave women the ballot. But for the most part, woman suffrage was not a popular political issue among women or men.

When Charlotte Woodward cast her vote (probably for Warren G. Harding, because he won by a landslide often credited to the huge number of women who voted for him) in November 1920, she took her place alongside millions of women who for the first time voted in a national election and experienced the power of their new status. They had prevailed.

"The right of citizens of the United States to vote shall not be denied or abridged by the United States or by any state on account of sex. Congress shall have power to enforce this article by appropriate legislation."

—U.S. Constitution, Nineteenth Amendment

7

WOMEN WERE IN THE WEST

by Natasha Tarpley

When I think about the West, the first images that come to mind are of calico dresses and bonnets, peppermint sticks and snow candy. As a child, I was an avid reader of the *Little House on the Prairie* books by Laura Ingalls Wilder. These books depicted the experiences of a family struggling to make a life on the western frontier (1871–85). As a little black girl in Chicago, it never occurred to me to wonder about the virtual invisibility of people who looked like me, and of Native Americans who lived on the Plains during that time. Instead, I was caught up in the vivid descriptions and the spirit of discovery that permeated the books and made even mundane tasks such as drawing water and building a fire seem like great adventures.

Eventually, I did ask questions, and I found some answers. I learned about the removal of Native Americans from their land; about African Americans who founded black towns; and, yes, about women, many of whom were single, who chose to go West for the adventure and the chance to become self-sufficient.

Below are three stories of three different western experiences that stand in sharp contrast to the simplified cowboy-and-Indian—and even *Little House*—version of the Old West.

INDIAN TERRITORY, 1838

Grace Cloud, an eleven-year-old Cherokee girl who is setting up camp with her family in what is now Oklahoma.

In the 1830s, with the Indian Removal Act, Congress created a huge new Indian Territory, which was to stretch from Texas to the middle Missouri River. Cherokee, Choctaw, Chickasaw, Creek, Seminole, and members of other Native American tribes were promised that this land would be theirs forever. Some ninety thousand men, women, and children disappeared from their lands in the Southeast and other parts of the country.

The Cherokee were among the last to go. Some agreed to move voluntarily. Others were forcibly removed from their homes and made to walk across country along the route that is now remembered as the Trail of Tears (1838–39).

But still, settlers from the South and East rushed to the territory that was supposed to be set aside for Native Americans. Many arrived by covered wagons along the popular route known as the Overland Trail. Others came by train, by ship, and even on foot.

Every evening, when it is time for night, a boy rides across the sky on his horse to draw down the sun. He rides to the four corners—north, south, east, west—and with the long, strong silver thread he carries in his pouch, he sews the sky shut like a big burlap sack, pulling the sun and all its colors inside. All that shows is the dark underbelly of the sky, a purple-black color, which I imagine is soft and smooth as tanned buffalo hide; and shiny silver dots, where the boy made his stitches. Sometimes he spreads them all over the sky with no order and sometimes he sews patterns and symbols. He makes a knot that keeps the sky closed. One day the knot is fat and round; another day, it is curved like a bow or a fingernail. In the morning, he will undo all of his handiwork in order to release the sun and capture it once again.

I have not told anyone about my friend in the sky, not even Mama. I am afraid that if I do, the whites will find out and take him away like they have taken our land and the things that once belonged to us. He is my constant companion. He has been with me since I was riding my mother's back. And he was with me on the long walk, when we had to leave our land and come to this new place. We walked until our feet turned to fire and then walked some more. My littlest sister could not walk anymore, so she laid down. But then she did not get up again. That night, the sky rider made a pattern that looked like a long rope with a bowl at the end. I believe my sister climbed inside and rode away with him on his horse. Maybe she will become a sky rider, too.

I don't know why this has happened. Why we had to move. Papa says the whites speak words that taste sweet on the outside, but are filled with poison. Our people swallowed too many of these words and the poison ate up our strength. Then the whites came and pointed their guns at us and made us walk the long walk to land that does not know our names. Soon the grass will grow over our old homeland and someone will turn the ground until all traces of us have disappeared. I do not like the feeling of disappearing. It is like being a ghost without a family to bless and send your spirit on. So you forever roam.

Tonight, the boy in the sky makes a pattern like an arrow, and where the arrow points, I dig a small hole. I plant my favorite beads for my sister, so that if she comes down from the sky she will know where her people are; she will know the way home.

OKLAHOMA, 1889

Nora Daley, a twenty-four-year-old Anglo-American woman who has just finished surveying her and her twenty-three-year-old sister's claim.

In 1862, Congress passed the Homestead Act in an effort to stimulate settlement of the western region. The law enabled anyone who was a United States citizen or intended to become one, and who was twenty-one years old or who was the head of a household, to file a claim for 160 acres of land. The act required homesteaders to pay a fourteen-dollar filing fee, and before they could receive title to the property they had to live on and improve the land for five years (later, three years).

On April 22, 1889, President Benjamin Harrison officially authorized the opening of unoccupied lands in the Indian Territory to settlers. At noon on that day, at the sounding of bugles and gunfire, almost one hundred thousand settlers surged forward to stake their claims in a massive rush for land.

The Homestead Act and the opening of unoccupied land are examples of the laws and government orders in place during the late 1800s and early 1900s that enabled free American women—single, divorced, and widowed—to own land in their own names.

Dear Mother,

Just a quick note to let you know your girls have arrived in Oklahoma in one piece. A bit weary from travel, but intact nonetheless. The train ride seemed endless. Full of stops and bumpy passages. But Sister and I persevered, and not without cheer. We amused ourselves watching the landscape go by and telling each other stories of all the adventures we will have in our new home. Our train car was packed with those like ourselves, eager for adventure, and full of hope for a new life. You could almost taste the excitement in the air. Sister and I met a lovely woman from Kansas, whose husband also has a claim in Oklahoma; perhaps she will be a neighbor to us.

Our train pulled in to Guthrie after nightfall. We were forced to spend the night at a boardinghouse, as there were no stagecoaches until morning. There was but one bed left, so we had to share. The terrible food made my stomach turn the whole night through. I must have gotten not more than 20 minutes sleep. Already I miss our comfortable home, my warm bed. . . . Enough of this, your girls have inherited your stubbornness, Mother, and your strength. We will go forward.

This morning, we went to the office of the man who would show us to our land. We took the bumpy coach ride about 15 miles east of Guthrie. All around us were people camped out in tents. When we reached our destination, we met the man whose brother sold us the land back in New York. He told us that when the government opened up the Indian land to settlers 5 months ago in April, there was a stampede. Must have been close to 100,000 people, he said, all rushing

to stake their claim at the sound of a gunshot that signaled the official opening of the land. We are fortunate that this man wanted to sell so soon, albeit at a much inflated price.

We are also fortunate that the owner had the fortitude to build a shack, so we shall not be consigned to the tents. Our dwelling is very plain. It has one room measuring eight feet by ten and two windows, one at either end. A stove in the middle of the room and a sturdy table with two steady chairs—a luxury! There is enough coal to start us off—thank goodness the weather has not turned cold.

But Mother, I am scared. I chose to come here to experience a new place, and for the chance to have something of my own. Now, I'm not so sure. I remember myself as a girl who could scarcely keep her feet on the ground with all the running and climbing and exploring I did. Where is that girl now? I fear she has run off and left a coward in her place. I say this to you from the privacy of my own heart. I will not let Sister see me this way. I came out back under the pretense of picking a spot for the garden. And yes, I have already planted a few tears.

Ah, but it is beautiful, Mother. The clear sky. And never have I seen so many stars or such a bright moon. As I was digging a bit in the soil, I came upon a curious thing: a handful of beads. I thought first that they were seeds, but their color is unlike any seed I know of. Blues and reds, yellow and orange, too. Very pretty, really. Perhaps this is my welcome. I shall keep them in a jar beside my bed to remind me of our arrival. And now, Mother, I bid you good night. I am off to sleep for the first time in my very own home.

Your loving daughter,
Nora

OKLAHOMA, 1894

Sophia Langston, a thirty-year-old black woman whose husband founded an all-black town.

My husband has sent me to survey this land, his latest purchase. He bought it

The pioneering life was tough on women homesteaders. These women, who came from a wide range of economic, ethnic, racial, and religious backgrounds, faced the challenge of making a new life out of nothing—literally. Many women arrived at their claims with nothing but what they could carry in their arms. They often had to build their own living quarters, figure out how to perform everyday tasks such as cooking and washing in an unfamiliar terrain, and work their land. Even women who settled in more established towns or communities had to adjust to new climates, as well as new people and social customs.

But as hard as life was for all women, it was perhaps doubly so for women of color. Black, Hispanic, Asian, and Native American women not only had to meet the physical and emotional demands of frontier living, they also shouldered the extra burden of racial discrimination.

Black women, many of whom left the South to escape racial persecution and slavery, often confronted similar discriminatory conditions out West. Many western cities and states barred blacks from using public transportation and recreational facilities, and even from attending white public schools. Blacks could not go to theaters or enter some department stores. They could not rent rooms in hotels or be served in restaurants outside of their communities. Blacks were even barred from traveling with some wagon trains over the Overland Trail to come west.

Hispanic, Asian, and Native American women faced these restrictions as well. These women also had to overcome language barriers, for many first-generation settlers and newer immigrants did not speak English.

In addition, the lives of Asian and Native Americans, in particular, continued to be regulated and restricted by the federal government. In 1882 the Chinese Exclusion Act was passed, which restricted the number of Chinese women that would be allowed into the United States. Those who were allowed in were detained for weeks and made to show evidence that they were not prostitutes.

Similarly, the government continued to pass laws to forcibly contain Native Americans on reservations. There was also a series of laws that prohibited certain cultural practices such as dancing and speaking native languages. Other acts, such as the Dawes Act of 1887 (also called the Allotment Act), undermined tribal structures and traditional gender roles by forcing Native Americans to adopt the nuclear family model and encouraging men to take over farming tasks. Consequently, many Native American women lost the tribal status and means of independence they had traditionally gained through their agricultural abilities.

To combat these obstacles, women of color had to rely on themselves and one another. Black settlers founded their own towns and communities, where women played major roles as teachers, businesspeople, and community leaders. Women of color also developed improvement societies, dedicated to instilling a sense of independence in their members. These women took on the role of educating their children and feeding the poor in their communities when the law barred them from schools and public services. They also created outlets for entertainment, since their people could not attend theaters or eat in restaurants.

Women of color became activists, speaking, writing, and fighting against the injustices their people faced. They also built bridges with white people, pushing back the boundaries of prejudice and ignorance to make the frontier a more hospitable place for all people.

cheap from two sisters, white women, who had to leave in a rush when one of them fell ill. He didn't want me to go, but there was no one else to send, everyone being so busy with the building of the town. Truthfully, I was happy to go. Oh, it feels so good to be on the open land again, away from all the hustle and bustle of planning and building. My husband, he has grand ideas. And I love him for that. In just a few years, he has turned this vastness into a place people are proud to call home, those who are willing to work hard, that is. My husband sees Oklahoma as the black man's nation: a place where colored people own all the land and businesses. He sends his agents down South to tell the people about our town, how nobody but coloreds live there, how even the title to the land couldn't pass to a white man. Coloreds for coloreds. And they have come, by the trainload and the wagonload, some on foot. All trying to escape the horrors of the South. Many are disappointed when they arrive and see just a few buildings, people still putting up their homes. But that's just fine, for it's the hardier stock that stays to work and make something for themselves.

Me, I am a simpler sort myself. Nothing makes me happier than to stick my bare feet into the warm earth, as I am doing now. My husband would have a fit. That is not proper conduct for the wife of a town founder, he would say. But I am a country girl at heart, he knew this when he married me. And even now, I would give it all up—the grand house my husband has planned, the little bakery I run in town, the literary society—for a chance to come back to the land.

Yet I remain firmly committed to the mission my husband and I share. I believe it is our duty as colored people to create a place where others of our kind can live in peace and prosper. Who else will do this important work but us? I hear that there are colored people, women at that, who have come by themselves and bought land, then have literally driven a wagon back and forth to bring others west. My heart is full of pride to be among that number who are pushing forward and clearing the way.

Well, it is almost nightfall. The wagon my husband is sending to collect me should be around soon. I have enough time to eat the small supper I packed. And I will have the treat of dining by sunset. A beautiful sight indeed.

While I was poking around the cabin, I found a jar of beads the sisters must have left behind, although they look more like a young girl's treasure. They are so bright and cheerful, I am tempted to take them for myself. But I have the feeling they belong here. I know my husband's men will tear down the cabin once the land is ready for settling. It seems a shame to leave the beads inside to be tossed away like rubbish. So I bury them here, in the soil. Perhaps they will bless the ground and allow our hopes and homes to flourish.

Despite the differences among the women who sought to make the West their own during the nineteenth and on into the twentieth centuries, they have left a common inheritance for us their daughters. They have given us the spirit of adventure; the ability to see far past the choices that are set before us and to envision more for our lives; courage and strength to keep searching, pushing back barriers and borders until we find what we are looking for. Best of luck in the discovery and exploration of your own frontiers.

by Suheir Hammad

U.S. WOMEN ARE DIVERSE

From the very beginning, the United States has been a nation of immigrants—forced and volunteer—and in the nineteenth and twentieth centuries the range of countries from which new immigrants have come has steadily expanded. As is the case with men, the process of becoming an American citizen has been one filled with anxiety for immigrant women, whether it was Chinese women in the mid-nineteenth century, or Western and Eastern European women in the late nineteenth/early twentieth century or African, Asian, South American, or West Indian women in the mid- and late twentieth century. These determined and persevering women acclimated themselves to a new and ever-evolving American culture while struggling to maintain an identity related to their own personal and cultural experiences.

While the following poem was written specifically for my mother, who came to the United States from a Palestinian refugee camp in Jordan in 1978, the cultural references can speak to a range of women and their experiences.

this is to certify that my mother is now natural

complexion   medium   certified
pickled and jarred into salsa   mild
not too sweet   not quite hot
not too black   not quite white

naturalized   medium
middle   mediocre

what was so middle about her
hands de-tangled
parted and quilted
thick black waves
into braids   rolled
grape leaves with style and speed
scrubbed ovens   knees   and backs of ears
clean with love
nails always looked neat
but on closer inspection   chipped
and tugged tired

what was mediocre about
her voice   screaming curses   shrill about
get up for school   singing um kolthom[4] to foreign ears
telling stories about owls
prophets and snakes
certified   citizen   natural   complexion   medium

how would hips be categorized
childbearing   too wide   average
or nose   indo-european   semitic   mediterranean
would your butt be your african
trait   eyes indian   hair mulatto
tongue arab

_____

4 An Egyptian singer (1904–75).

mama you natural
woman of sun water and air
given a nation
though no land
through a piece of paper thin

palestinian woman
loss embroidered on your forehead

more than tabbouleh   children   husband
and thin ass pieces of paper
which can never jar your style
essence   warmth
never certify your nature
your particular humor
aspirations   dreams   heartbreaks

you can make vegans eat your lamb
with relish   rip your heart out
to feed your man you who
make rhinestones sparkle diamonds
sequin your daughters' ears with your laugh

you memorized
but did not have
dead presidents backwards and forwards
for citizenship   a place to lay
your head but always told us
take me home when i'm dead

woman natural
medium middle to nothing
never can they certify
what they don't understand

9

The Legacy of Wise Words

by Rosalie Maggio

From the beginning of time, women have been as quotable as men. Not that you'd know this. For the longest time women's words were very rarely quoted. Even quotation books ignored them for centuries. In the 1980 edition of *Bartlett's Familiar Quotations*, for example, only 1/2 of 1% of the quotations were by women.

In 1977, Elaine Partnow (who counted those quotes in *Bartlett's*) published the first collection of quotations by women. She opened the door to a dazzling wealth of clever, memorable, wise, and humorous words by women. Since then, things have been getting better, although in the 1992 edition of *Bartlett's*, only 5.5% of the quoted lines were written by women. Mathwise, that means 94.5% of *Bartlett's* consists of men's words.

When I noticed that a Minneapolis newspaper's "Quote of the Day" averaged one quotation by a woman for every fourteen quotations by men, I wrote suggesting they even things up.

After my letter appeared, a man wrote to me, explaining that the reason for those figures was that "women have never said, written, or uttered anything worth quoting."

Oh?

In addition to being a victim of redundancy ("said" and "uttered" meaning the same thing, of course), he was a victim of circular thinking: he knew that women were not quoted because they had never said anything worth quoting and he knew they had never said anything worth quoting because they were not quoted.

Women have always had a great many astonishing, beautiful, and thought-provoking things to say. The problem has been that the people (well, okay, the men) who compiled the quotation books didn't include them.

Today we have more collections of quotations by women, and the percentage of women's words in other collections is increasing. The next time you want to add sparkle to an essay or paper with a quotation, check out what women have had to say on your subject. (You'll be helping keep women's words as visible as men's!) Here's a small sampling of the gems that await you.

This world taught woman nothing skillful and then said her work was valueless. It permitted her no opinions and said she did not know how to think. It forbade her to speak in public, and said the sex had no orators.
—suffragist and educator Carrie Chapman Catt in *The History of Woman Suffrage* (vol. 4, 1902), edited by Susan B. Anthony and Ida Husted Harper.

I am not belittling the brave pioneer men, but the sunbonnet as well as the sombrero has helped to settle this glorious land of ours.
—novelist Edna Ferber in *Cimarron* (1930).

Whatever we do to any other thing in the great web of life, we do to ourselves, for we are one.
—Crow poet and ceremonial leader Brooke Medicine Eagle in *Buffalo Woman Comes Singing* (1991).

Some leaders are born women.
—politician (and former candidate for vice president) Geraldine A. Ferraro in her speech "The Future of Women in Politics" (1991).

I can't change my sex. But you can change your policy.
—journalist and foreign correspondent Helen Kirkpatrick (1940), on being told a newspaper didn't have women on its foreign affairs staff, in *Women of the World* (1988) by Julia Edwards.

One can never consent to creep when one feels an impulse to soar.
—suffragist, educator, and humanitarian Helen Keller in *The Story of My Life* (1902).

A popular saying in Alderson went as follows: "They work us like a horse, feed us like a bird, treat us like a child, dress us like a man—and then expect us to act like a lady."
—labor activist Elizabeth Gurley Flynn ("the Rebel Girl") in *The Alderson Story: My Life as a Political Prisoner* (1963).

We're half the people; we should be half the Congress.
—Congressional Representative Jeannette Rankin in *Jeannette Rankin* (1974) by Hannah Josephson.

When you get to the end of your rope—tie a knot in it and hang on.
—First Lady Eleanor Roosevelt in *You Learn by Living* (1960).

Sexism goes so deep that at first it's hard to see; you think it's just reality.
—activist-writer Alix Kates Shulman in *Burning Questions* (1978).

Language is also a place of struggle.
—cultural critic bell hooks in *Talking Back* (1989).

Those who have been required to memorize the world as it is will never create the world as it might be.
—writer Judith Groch in *The Right to Create* (1969).

We cannot legislate equality but we can legislate . . . equal opportunity for all.
—Congressional Representative Helen Gahagan Douglas in *A Full Life* (1982).

Getting what you go after is success; but liking it while you are getting it is happiness.
—writer Bertha Damon in *A Sense of Humus* (1943).

I think the reward for conformity is that everyone likes you except yourself.
—writer Rita Mae Brown in *Bingo* (1988).

Mama exhorted her children at every opportunity to "jump at de sun." We might not land on the sun, but at least we would get off the ground.
—writer and anthropologist Zora Neale Hurston in *Dust Tracks on a Road* (1942).

It is not easy to find happiness in ourselves, and it is not possible to find it elsewhere.
—historian and social critic Agnes Repplier in *Agnes Repplier* (1957) by Emma Repplier.

When you can't see straight ahead, it's because you're about to turn a corner.
—writer Myrtle Reed in *Old Rose and Silver* (1909).

What we call failure is not the falling down, but the staying down.
—actor Mary Pickford in *Reader's Digest* (1979).

Revenge leads to an empty fullness, like eating dirt.
—writer and humorist Mignon McLaughlin in *The Neurotic's Notebook* (1963).

I like people who refuse to speak until they are ready to speak.
—playwright Lillian Hellman in *An Unfinished Woman* (1969).

Everybody gets so much information all day long that they lose their common sense.
—writer Gertrude Stein (1946) in *Gertrude Stein: Her Life and Work* (1957) by Elizabeth Sprigge.

If you're going to generalize about women, you'll find yourself up to here in exceptions.
—writer Dolores Hitchens in *In a House Unknown* (1973).

The next best thing to being clever is being able to quote some one who is.
—writer Mary Pettibone Poole in *A Glass Eye at a Keyhole* (1938).

by Marsha Weinstein

The Landmarks of Our Lives

The Suffrage Statue in the Rotunda of the Capitol Building . . . the Sewall-Belmont House in Washington, D.C., once the headquarters of the National Woman's Party . . . the Vietnam Women's Memorial Project (also in D.C.) . . . the Sojourner Truth Memorial in Battle Creek, Michigan. In small-town and big-city America, there are visible tributes, memorials, and other remembrances of brave and noble women who made important contributions to our society—sites that can inspire us to do likewise.

It is true that there are far more public and private statues, homes, buildings, and streets revering men than women. According to the National Register of Historic Places, there are approximately 9,800 sites commemorating important people, but only 360 are of women. And since there's a Boy Scouts memorial (in Washington, D.C.), shouldn't there be one for the Girl Scouts?

This is why we need to remember those sites that do pay tribute to women's creations, innovations, crusades, and adventures. So when you're visiting another city or knocking about your own hometown, do a little site-seeking and sight-seeing of women's achievements. Here's a small peek at some of what you'll find.

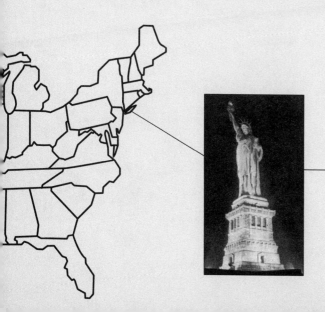

• Emma Lazarus was a famous Jewish poet who wrote the sonnet "The New Colossus" (1883), which is engraved on a tablet inside the base of the Statue of Liberty. ". . . Give me your tired, your poor, Your huddled masses yearning to breathe free. . . ."

• This statue of Sacagawea in Bismarck, North Dakota, is one of several in America that celebrates the brave Shoshone woman who served as guide and interpreter for the 1805 Lewis and Clark expedition. Sacagawea accompanied the expedition up the Missouri River and across the Rocky Mountains to the Pacific Ocean in Oregon and back to her Mandan village, located on the Missouri River.

• Madame Walker Theatre Center at 617 Indiana Avenue in Indianapolis, Indiana. When erected in 1927, this was the Walker Building, national headquarters of the cosmetics empire founded by the epic Madame C. J. Walker. The Walker Building was the brainchild of Madame's daughter, A'Lelia Walker.

• The Willa Cather Pioneer Memorial in Red Cloud, Nebraska (a.k.a. "Catherland"), celebrates the Pulitzer Prize–winning author who used Red Cloud as the setting for many of her books (among them *My Antonia, The Song of the Lark,* and *O Pioneers!*). Inscribed on this historical marker are these words: "The history of every country begins in the heart of a man or a woman. The history of this land began in the heart of Willa Cather."

• Wendover (132 Frontier Nursing Service Drive, Wendover, Kentucky) is the national headquarters of the Frontier Nursing Service, established in 1925 by Mary Breckinridge to provide health care for the poor. Breckenridge is credited with training the first professional nurse-midwives.

• The Kate Mullaney House at 350 Eighth Street in Troy, New York, was home, for a time (1869–1875), to the Irish immigrant Kate Mullaney, who, in 1864, at the age of nineteen, organized the all-female Collar Laundry Union along with a co-worker (Esther Keegan). On July 15, 1998, First Lady Hillary Rodham Clinton did the honors of officially declaring Mullaney's home a national historic landmark.

• Now a museum, the Maria Mitchell House (One Vestal Street, Nantucket Island, Massachusetts) was the childhood home of the librarian and self-taught astronomer Maria Mitchell (1818–89), who was the first American to record a comet sighting (1847), the first female professor of astronomy (1865–89, at Vassar), and the first woman elected to the Academy of Arts and Sciences (1848) and the American Philosophical Society (1869).

• This hundred-foot-long waterwall, inscribed with the historic "Declaration of Sentiments" and the names of its signers, is at Fall and Water streets in the Women's Rights National Historical Park (created in 1980) in Seneca Falls, New York.

• Alva Smith Vanderbilt Belmont Mausoleum (Woodlawn Cemetery, Bronx, New York) is the final resting place of the wealthy socialite and feminist who used her money to support the suffrage movement. A suffrage banner hangs inside the mausoleum.

• The Mary McLeod Bethune Memorial in Washington, D.C.'s Lincoln Park (at Thirteenth and East Capitol streets) honors the founder of what is today Bethune-Cookman College (Daytona Beach, Florida), founder of the National Council of Negro Women, and adviser to President Franklin Delano Roosevelt and Eleanor Roosevelt (as well as her good friend).

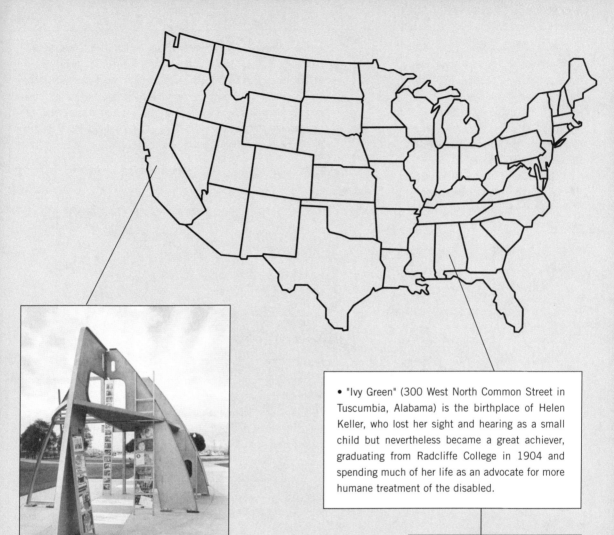

• "Ivy Green" (300 West North Common Street in Tuscumbia, Alabama) is the birthplace of Helen Keller, who lost her sight and hearing as a small child but nevertheless became a great achiever, graduating from Radcliffe College in 1904 and spending much of her life as an advocate for more humane treatment of the disabled.

• The Rosie the Riveter Memorial in Richmond, California, designed by Susan Schwartzenberg and Cheryl Barton, pays tribute to women's war-effort work during World War II. This 400-foot-long stainless steel sculpture, which evokes a ship's hull under construction, includes "image ladders" and etched granite paving stones that contain a time line and women's memories of the era. The memorial is located in the Rosie the Riveter Memorial Park, once the site of the Kaiser Shipyards.

STEP INSIDE . . .

Here's a list of some museums that are definitely worth your while.

- International Women's Air and Space Museum (Cleveland, Ohio)
- National Cowgirl Museum and Hall of Fame (Fort Worth, Texas)
- National First Ladies' Library–Saxton McKinley House (Canton, Ohio)
- National Museum of Women in the Arts (Washington, D.C.)
- National Women's Hall of Fame (Seneca Falls, New York)
- Women in Military Service for America Memorial (Arlington National Cemetery, Washington, D.C.)
- Women of the West Museum (Denver, Colorado)
- The Women's Museum: An Institute for the Future (Dallas, Texas)
- Women's Rights National Historical Park (Seneca Falls, New York)

Stay on the lookout. There are many other great museums, including more than a few that exist only in cyberspace, such as the Jewish Women's Archive and the National Museum of Women's History.

For armchair traveling, check out . . .

- *Western Women: Their Land, Their Lives,* edited by Lillian Schlissel, Vicki L. Puiz, and Janice Monk (1988).
- *Susan B. Anthony Slept Here: A Guide to American Women's Landmarks* by Lynn Sherr and Jurate Kazickas (1994)

TAKE ACTION!

Interested in joining the campaign to increase the number of women's history sites? If so, obtain a copy of *Women's History Is Everywhere: 10 Ideas for Celebrating in Communities, A How-To Community Handbook,* prepared by the President's Commission on the Celebration of Women in American History. Write to the U.S. General Services Administration, Department of Communications, 1800 F Street N.W., Washington, D.C. 20405. You can also get this as a PDF file off the Web: http://hydra.gsa.gov/staff/pa/whchandbook.pdf

In this booklet, you'll find great ideas (and tips on how to follow through on them). For example: "Create Community Women's History Trails: Develop a Map of Local Women's History Sites" and "Build a Cooperative Community Project: Design and Place Historic Markers."

"Don't Agon

Written and illustrated by Ann Decker

They were taken for granted and confined as unpaid labor in the home. They were deprived of education and opportunity and told to leave the political and economic world to men.

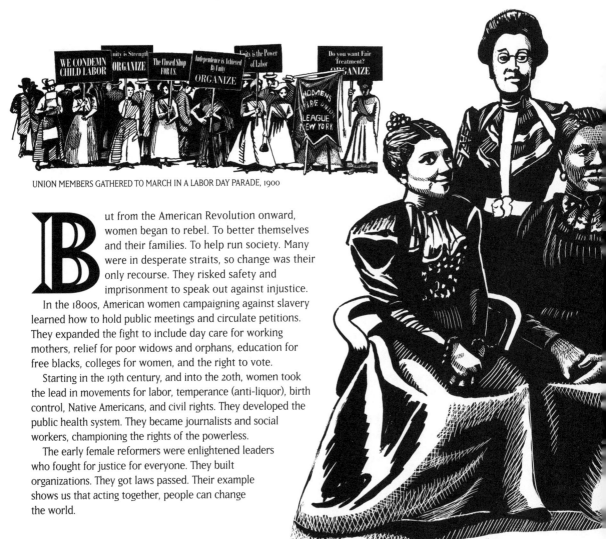

UNION MEMBERS GATHERED TO MARCH IN A LABOR DAY PARADE, 1900

But from the American Revolution onward, women began to rebel. To better themselves and their families. To help run society. Many were in desperate straits, so change was their only recourse. They risked safety and imprisonment to speak out against injustice.

In the 1800s, American women campaigning against slavery learned how to hold public meetings and circulate petitions. They expanded the fight to include day care for working mothers, relief for poor widows and orphans, education for free blacks, colleges for women, and the right to vote.

Starting in the 19th century, and into the 20th, women took the lead in movements for labor, temperance (anti-liquor), birth control, Native Americans, and civil rights. They developed the public health system. They became journalists and social workers, championing the rights of the powerless.

The early female reformers were enlightened leaders who fought for justice for everyone. They built organizations. They got laws passed. Their example shows us that acting together, people can change the world.

ize, Organize!"

—FLORYNCE KENNEDY

THE INDUSTRIAL REVOLUTION
(1750–1850) By 1800, steam-powered machines dominated English industry. Craftsmen gave way to a "division of labor," in which each worker made only 1 part, and a collection of workers made up an "assembly line," housed in a factory. Feudalism's 3 classes—nobility, clergy, and commons—gave way to capitalism's 2 classes—management and labor. The factory system came to America. The steamboat (1807) made shipping faster and cheaper, creating a demand for more goods—and larger factories. Cities grew up to house armies of workers, including thousands of immigrants. Women and children were for the first time hired for unskilled jobs outside the home. By 1830, in response to long hours, low pay, and unhealthy conditions, they began to protest. Thus began the long, concerted effort by women activists to raise their standard of living, to improve their lives.

AFRICAN AMERICAN OFFICERS OF THE WOMEN'S LEAGUE, 1900

THE CIVIL WAR (1861–65) AND AFTER
During the Crimean War in Europe (1853–56), England's Florence Nightingale showed that female nurses could work near a battleground, so in America's Civil War the Union army recruited 3,000 frontline nurses. After the Civil War, industry boomed and women took on new kinds of jobs: domestic servants, garment workers, printers, umbrella makers, and even cigar rollers! But women earned half as much as men. They got no support from upper-class women fighting for the vote—the suffragists. And labor unions took only men. Then Philadelphia's Knights of Labor (1878) decided to build their strength by including all working people. They expanded nationally and recruited women and blacks. One of their demands is still an issue today: equal pay for equal work.

The stories of a few speak for many

Mental health pioneer

DOROTHEA DIX (1802–87) was a teacher in pre–Civil War
Boston who was inspired by the ferment of reform centered
around abolition. In 1841, she volunteered to teach Sunday
school in a prison and discovered convicts who were mentally ill,
shivering in unheated rooms. Her efforts over the next 40 years
helped to build 32 hospitals for the mentally ill.

"Angel of the battlefield"

CLARA BARTON
(1821–1912) began
teaching at age 15.
During the Civil War,
she secured supplies
and nursed soldiers.
Appointed
Superintendent of
Nurses for the Union by
Lincoln, she founded the
American branch of the
International Red Cross in 1881.

"Pray for the dead and *fight like hell* for the living."

—MOTHER JONES

Early and unique labor leader

MARY HARRIS "MOTHER" JONES (1830–1930) lost her ironworker husband and 2 children in a yellow fever epidemic in 1867. Then in 1871, her dressmaking business burned up in the Great Chicago Fire. Desolate and alone, she turned her empathy into action by fighting for others. As a union organizer, she led workers in using group pressure for better wages and working conditions, especially for children and miners, like those pictured below. In 1905, she was one of the founders of the Industrial Workers of the World (IWW). She was fiery and fearless well into her 80s.

"It's great to fight for

TRIANGLE SHIRTWAIST FACTORY FIRE

In 1909, seamstresses in the shirtwaist (blouse) factories of New York organized a strike for better conditions. They were fired. Thousands rallied around the strikers, including, for the first time, upper-class women and male workers. The strike was settled, but nothing was done to improve the workers' safety. Then 2 years later, in New York City, 146 workers, mostly women, were killed by a fire at the Triangle Shirtwaist Factory. Their escape doors locked, many leapt to their death from the upper-floor windows. This disaster horrified the nation and forced the passing of stricter laws to protect workers.

freedom with a "Rebel Girl"

—JOE HILL

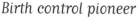
After a cartoon by John Sloan. 1911.

THE PROGRESSIVE ERA (1890–1920)

During this period of unprecedented industrial growth, the United States became the richest nation on earth. Blacks from the South, Europeans, and Russians migrated to northern American cities to fill the increased demand for labor and were forced to endure brutal living conditions. Many women activists fought to offset the tremendous political and economic power of the corporations, some through charity and reforms, others through direct action in labor unions and new political parties. Progressive Party women revitalized the suffrage (women's vote) movement. Progressivism, populism, socialism, communism, anarchism—it was the era of "isms," all fighting to defend the worker's interests against those of government and big business.

"The Rebel Girl"

ELIZABETH GURLEY FLYNN (1890–1964) was the daughter of working-class socialists. She left high school to be a full-time union speaker and fund-raiser. She traveled the country for the IWW, organizing strikes of textile workers and miners, and was often arrested. In 1920, she was a co-founder of the American Civil Liberties Union. In later years, she joined the Communist Party and became chairman of the CPUSA from 1961 to 1964.

Birth control pioneer

MARGARET SANGER (1879–1966), a nurse on Manhattan's Lower East Side, found that her patients were too poor to support their large families. Infant mortality was high and mothers often died in childbirth or from botched illegal abortions. Committed to the right of every woman to avoid an unwanted pregnancy, she was jailed in 1914 for publicizing the facts about birth control. In 1916, Sanger started the first U.S. birth control clinic, in Brooklyn, and for this served 30 days in a Queens jail. But the harassment backfired, polarizing public opinion in her favor. Her appeals forced federal courts to legalize access to information about birth control. The organization she founded in 1921 and ran for many years grew into the International Planned Parenthood Federation.

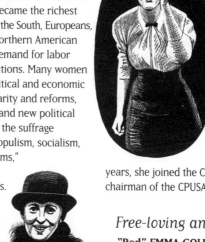

Free-loving anarchist

"Red" EMMA GOLDMAN (1869–1940), a Russian immigrant, worked in East Coast clothing factories, where among her fellow workers she found socialists and anarchists. She became a spirited public speaker, agitating for social reform, free speech, birth control, and "free love." Fiery and romantic, she was jailed for obscenity and inciting to riot. She founded the magazine *Mother Earth*, published from 1906 to 1917. Emma and other radicals opposed U.S. involvement in World War I. They believed that patriotism was just an excuse to make ordinary people fight and die for the interests of wealthy governments. Eventually, the U.S. government deported her back to Russia.

The most dangerous

Leading reformer

JANE ADDAMS (1860–1935) founded the famous Hull House in a crowded immigrant neighborhood in Chicago in 1889. It was a community center where people could take college-level classes, socialize, use the nursery, playground, gymnasium, and kitchen. It included many buildings and was a hub of activity where reformers gathered and worked. The idea for community centers like this originated in England. In America, it was here that the first social workers got their training, and where the fields of social work and public health began. The list of Addams's causes is long. Her work for labor reform, for immigrants and civil rights, and for suffrage resulted in many of the standards of decency we take for granted in the workplace. Addams, for her opposition to World War I, was called "the most dangerous woman in America" in the tabloids of her day. She was awarded the Nobel Peace Prize in 1931.

Public health pioneer

LILLIAN WALD (1859–1932) was a nurse who began to work with the poor on Manhattan's Lower East Side. Because conditions were wretched, in 1895 she opened a nurse's settlement that grew into the first visiting nurses association and the innovative Henry Street Settlement House. It still exists today.

Workers' advocate

FLORENCE KELLEY (1859–1932) was influenced by European socialism as a young woman. While living at Hull House in Chicago, she investigated conditions in sweatshops and tenements that resulted in legislation to improve labor conditions. She moved to New York to join the Henry Street Settlement and then became a lawyer. In 1899, she became general secretary of the National Consumers League.

women in America?

A VISITING NURSE FROM THE HENRY STREET SETTLEMENT WITH HER PATIENTS ON NEW YORK'S LOWER EAST SIDE

Corporate watchdog

IDA TARBELL (1857–1944) was a college-educated writer who supported her graduate studies at the Sorbonne in Paris by writing for American magazines. Her 1902 journalistic exposé of Standard Oil for *McClure's* magazine is one of the most thorough accounts of a business monopoly and its unfair practices ever written. The articles also helped to define the growing trend of investigation and crusading in liberal journals of the day which came to be known as muckraking, in which journalists acted as the public conscience.

Civil rights pioneer

IDA B. WELLS (1862–1931) was the daughter of slaves, but was born free. She became a teacher and later a journalist. About 60 years before the modern civil rights movement, Wells brought a suit against the Chesapeake and Ohio Railroad for removing her from her seat in the whites-only section of a train. She lost the suit, but that didn't stop her. After 3 friends were lynched by a mob, she began an editorial campaign as a writer for the *New York Age* against the widespread lynching of blacks. Her offices were ransacked. But that didn't stop her. She expanded her crusade by organizing anti-lynching societies. Wells also founded the first black women's suffrage group, the Alpha Suffrage Club.

Undercover investigator

NELLIE BLY (1867–1922) had no formal schooling, but she became the best-known journalist of her day. She was hired as a writer on a newspaper when she wrote an angry letter to the editor in response to an article entitled "What Are Girls Good For?" Born Elizabeth Cochran, she took her pen name from a popular song. Her first articles concerned the conditions of slum dwellers and working girls in Pittsburgh. As a writer for the *New York World*, she got herself admitted to Blackwell's Asylum on what is now Roosevelt Island in New York City by pretending to be insane. Her exposé of conditions there brought about improvements in patient care. Similar exploits took her into sweatshops and jails.

UNION DELEGATES GATHERED TO SUPPORT STRIKING WORKERS IN 1913.
A scab is a person who breaks a strike by replacing a striking worker on the job.

FROM WORLD WAR I TO THE PRESENT (1914–2002)

When World War I broke out in Europe in 1914, America experienced a period of extreme patriotism. Government and business interests feared the social upheaval caused by the Russian Revolution would spread. American activists were hounded and jailed, inhibiting organizing efforts. Furthermore, when women finally got the right to vote in 1920, many activists retired from the fray with a sigh of relief.

America didn't experience another surge of activism until the Great Depression that began in 1929. From that time through World War II to the present, periods of conservative backlash have followed ones of progressive reform and institution building. But some women continued to agitate for peace, civil rights, child welfare, and educational advancement despite many obstacles. In doing so, they laid the groundwork for the social movements of the 1960s and 1970s.

Today, women continue to press for gender equality. They're still members and leaders of the labor movement in the U.S. They demonstrate and work on behalf of foreign workers in countries where American business has gone to find cheap labor. And they've championed new causes: gay, Indian, and animal rights, environmental safety, and gun control, just to name a few, by following in the footsteps of the women who came before them.

As we go marching, marching
We bring the greater days.
The rising of the woman
is the rising of the race.
No more the drudge or idler—
Ten that toil while one reposes.
But a sharing of life's glories:
                    Bread and roses!
                    Bread and roses!"

— JAMES OPPENHEIM, 1912

For centuries, women have known that though they might be denied power individually, when they band together nothing can stop them. From Lucretia Mott's American Equal Rights Association, AWSA[5], NWSA[6], NAWSA[7], and the National Women's Party to the National Organization for Women (NOW), women's organizations have long provided women with a sounding board *and* a springboard, a place to share inspiration and ideas—and a voice loud enough to make those ideas heard. As Robin Morgan, founder of the first international women's think tank and former editor-in-chief of *Ms.* magazine, proclaimed in the title of her 1970 book, *Sisterhood Is Powerful.* Here are just a few of the ways our feisty and fearless foremothers have used the power of sisterhood to change the world for you and me.

The Factory Girls Association: In the 19th century, the mills in Lowell, Massachusetts, offered unprecedented opportunities for women and girls of rural New England. In return for long hours and hard work, factory girls could earn more than they would be able to in traditional women's occupations and could get a taste of independence at a time when most women went directly from their parents' home to their husband's. Once they were hired, factory girls entered a community of women, living together, eating together, and working together. The solidarity created by this community spurred them to go on strike in 1834, when their wages were cut. The initial strike failed, but they went on strike again in 1836 and formed the Factory Girls Association, with Sarah Bagley emerging as one of their key voices. Under her leadership, the Factory Girls Association reorganized as the Lowell Female Labor Reform Association in 1844 and became the leading labor advocate in Lowell. The group expanded into other mill towns as well.

---

5 American Woman Suffrage Association.
6 National Woman Suffrage Association.
7 National American Woman Suffrage Association.

by Shana Corey

Young Women's Christian Association: During the Industrial Revolution, many people were worried about the moral fate of girls leaving their homes for the first time and going to work in the cities. The YWCA began in England as a movement to provide clean housing, wholesome recreation, and health information for the factory girls. The first United States organization opened in New York in 1858, and by the turn of the century there were hundreds of YWCAs throughout the U.S. The YWCA now has a membership of more than 2 million. Its mission is to eliminate racism and to empower women and girls.

Girls Clubs: The first Girls Club opened in Waterbury, Connecticut, in 1864 in order to provide a safe gathering place for factory girls and the daughters of mill workers. In the following decades, Girls Clubs popped up throughout the Northeast, and in 1945 nineteen Girls Clubs met and established the Girls Clubs of America. In 1990, the organization changed its name to Girls Inc. Girls Inc. works to prevent teenage pregnancy, fosters girls' interest in math and science, and encourages girls to reevaluate the messages media and society throw at them. Its mission is to inspire girls to be "strong, smart, and bold."

Women's Educational and Industrial Union:
Dr. Harriet Clisby, one of America's first female doctors, founded the WEIU in Boston in 1877. The union's early members included author Louisa May Alcott and other prominent Bostonians. Its purpose was to help poor immigrant women support themselves and their families. It ran a store that sold goods women produced, offered legal and employment counseling, and later added courses in dressmaking, housekeeping, and salesmanship. In 1910, the WEIU set up an appointment bureau to help find jobs for the growing number of female college graduates. (Aviator Amelia Earhart was one of the many women who sought employment help there.) The WEIU continues to advocate for women's educational and economic opportunities today.

Association of Collegiate Alumnae: In the

1880s and 1890s, several state universities opened their doors to women and the Seven Sisters colleges were founded (Mount Holyoke, Wellesley, Smith, Vassar, Bryn Mawr, Radcliffe, and Barnard). Few professions welcomed women, though, and many women graduated college only to be disappointed by their career options. In 1881, seventeen women decided that a group needed to be formed to promote higher education for women and provide alumnae with a network of women in similar situations. Sixty-five women came to the first meeting. The organization grew, and in 1921 it became known as the American Association of University Women. The AAUW now has more than 150,000 members and is known for its groundbreaking research on how women learn.

Woman's Era Club: Josephine St. Pierre Ruffin and other

African American Boston clubwomen organized the Woman's Era Club in 1893 in order to fight negative stereotypes about black women. The Woman's Era Club published the first black women's paper in the United States, *The Woman's Era*. In 1895, it called a national meeting of more than twenty African American women's clubs. That meeting led to the formation of the National Federation of Afro-American Women, whose purpose, Ruffin said, would be "to teach an ignorant and suspicious world that our aims and interests are identical to all good aspiring women."

National Council of Jewish Women:

Hannah G. Solomon called for the formation of an organization of Jewish women at the 1893 Columbian Exposition in Chicago. The council became an early proponent of the birth control movement and continues to support reproductive and individual freedoms today. The NCJW recently launched a national campaign called StoP (Strategies to Prevent Domestic Violence) and works to improve the lives of women and their families.

National Association of Colored Women:

This group was founded in Washington, D.C., in 1896 with the merger of the National Federation of Afro-American Women and the National League of Colored Women. Its founders included Harriet Tubman, Ida Bell Wells-Barnett, and Mary Church Terrell. Under Terrell's leadership, the club was active in establishing day-care centers and kindergartens and in fighting discrimination. It endorsed women's suffrage in 1912, two years before the General Federation of Women's Clubs (which did not allow black women). In 1958, the organization changed its name to the National Association of Colored Women's Clubs. Today the NACWC focuses on job training and equal pay. Its motto is "Lifting as we climb."

Women's Trade Union League:

Formed in 1903, after a meeting of the American Federation of Labor made it clear that women were not a priority for that organization, the WTUL worked for an eight-hour workday, minimum wages for women, women's suffrage, and equal pay for equal work. The league welcomed women of all social classes. During strikes, wealthier members were able to support their working-class sisters financially and by using their education and resources to communicate issues to the public.

American Home Economics Association:

Ellen Swallow Richards, one of the founding members of the Association of Collegiate Alumnae and author of *The Chemistry of Cooking and Cleaning* (1882) and *Sanitation in Daily Life* (1907), was elected as the organization's first president. In the 1990s, the group changed its name to the American Association of Family and Consumer Sciences (AAFCS) to better reflect changes in society and its mission.

Girl Scouts of America:

Juliette Gordon Low formed America's first troop of Girl Guides in Savannah, Georgia, in March 1912. The organization was modeled after the Boy Scouts and the Girl Guides of England. In 1915, the name was officially changed to the Girl Scouts. By

1919, when Low represented the United States in the world's first International Council of Girl Guides and Girl Scouts, there were troops in almost every state. Today millions of girls have been involved in the Girl Scouts, and the organization continues to promote self-reliance, independence, and service. The Girl Scouts are known for their annual cookie sale, which they've been conducting since 1936.

Heterodoxy: This New York–based club formed in 1912 for the purpose of giving professional women a place to express and listen to untraditional (heterodox) ideas without fear of censure. The club also became a gathering place for New York's feminist and lesbian culture. To ensure members' freedom of expression, Heterodoxy's meeting places and minutes were never recorded. Members included choreographer Agnes de Mille and writer Charlotte Perkins Gilman, author of "The Yellow Wallpaper" and *Herland*.

American Medical Women's Association: This association (originally the Medical Women's National Association) was founded in Chicago in 1915, a time when there were very few women doctors, in order to promote women's advancement in the field of medicine and put women physicians in touch with each other. Today AMWA includes 10,000 women physicians and medical students. It is a leading advocate for women's health, is active in forming national health care policy, and works to educate consumers and medical professionals about women's health issues. AMWA's current priorities are reproductive rights, universal health care, smoking prevention, and fighting violence against women.

League of Women Voters: Carrie Chapman Catt proposed forming a League of Women Voters to help women carry out their newly won responsibilities by educating them about the issues and encouraging informed participation in the political process. The League was officially established in 1920, after the passage of the Nineteenth Amendment. For many years, the LWV was known for sponsoring presidential debates. Today the League continues its work by educating and registering voters.

National Federation of Business and Professional Women's Clubs:
This organization was formed in 1919 to encourage women in the professions and white-collar jobs. One of its primary concerns was the right of married women to remain in the workforce. It was also an early supporter of the Equal Rights Amendment. Today, renamed Business and Professional Women/USA, it continues to be an advocate for working women and lobbies for the appointment of women to high-level government positions.

The Ninety-Nines:
In the 1920s, female pilots weren't allowed to compete in races with men, so they had their own race, the National Women's Air Derby (dubbed the Powder Puff Derby). After the 1929 race, several female pilots met and decided to form an organization to promote women's opportunities in aviation. They sent out invitations to all 117 licensed female pilots in the United States and, at Amelia Earhart's suggestion, decided to name the fledgling organization after the number of women who replied. Today the Ninety-Nines' original membership of 99 has grown to 6,500 women in 35 countries.

National Council of Negro Women:
Mary McLeod Bethune founded the NCNW in 1935 in order to unite African American women's groups into a collective political force. Bethune was elected the first president and remained in office until 1949. Mary Church Terrell, of the National Association for Colored Women, also held a leadership position. Today the NCNW numbers 4 million women and houses the National Archives for Black Women's History.

Daughters of Bilitis:
Founded in San Francisco in 1955, this group was the first major lesbian organization in the United States. The Daughters of Bilitis took their name from *Chansons de Bilitis*, the Sapphic love poems of Pierre Louys. They worked through education and legal reform to earn lesbians acceptance into mainstream American culture. The Daughters of Bilitis also published *The Ladder* magazine, an important resource for the gay and lesbian liberation movement.

La Leche League: In 1956, when bottle-feeding babies was the norm, a group of young mothers began to meet in order to support each other's decision to breast-feed. The organization adopted the name "La Leche" (from the Spanish word for "milk") because using the word "breast" wouldn't have been acceptable at the time. Over the past several decades, the La Leche League has started chapters all around the world. It currently has 40,000 members and offers telephone counseling, mothers' networks, and programs to increase awareness of breast-feeding's benefits.

Beyond NOW

NOW, founded in 1966, is the best-known women's rights organization in the world. Women didn't stop organizing with NOW, though. The late 1960s saw the rise of women's liberation, with groups such as New York Radical Women, Radical Lesbians, and Redstockings. The 1970s saw an explosion of organizing that cut across class and color lines, with the National Women's Political Caucus (founded by NOW's Betty Friedan and Representative Shirley Chisholm); MANA, a national Latina organization; Billie Jean King's Women's Sports Foundation; the National Coalition Against Domestic Violence; and the Coalition of Labor Union Women. The boom continued through the 1980s and 1990s with the Feminist Majority Foundation; the National Black Women's Health Project; Hispanas Organized for Political Equality (HOPE); and the National Asian Women's Health Organization. Groups such as the National Association of At-Home Mothers connected women in their homes, and international groups such as the Global Fund for Women reached across oceans.

How will organizations change the world in the 21st century? It's up to you. Join your local Girls Inc., revive Heterodoxy, or if you don't find something here that inspires you, organize a brand-new club. After all, what you do today is tomorrow's women's history.

13

LABOR PAINS HAVE BEEN INTENSE

by Safiya Henderson-Holmes

Although America indeed has founding fathers and mothers, many of the workers of the early 1900s and much later, especially in the factories of industrial America, were young people–teenagers–girls–boys. My poem below, "rituals of spring" (1989), commemorates a tragedy in one such factory in New York City, where girls and young women worked way beyond their dreams. "rituals of spring" is also a story of hope: of getting a job, having a place to live, and if you're very blessed, someone to love. This hope dug deep into the hearts of these young factory workers. This hope continues to bloom in America every spring.

from bareness to fullness flowers do bloom
whenever, however spring enters a room
oh, whenever, however spring enters a room

march 25th, 1911
at the triangle shirtwaist factory
a fire claimed the lives of 146 people, mostly women,
mostly children in the plume of their lives,
in the room of their lives
begging for spring, toiling and begging for spring

and in my head
as i read the history, afraid to touch the pictures
i imagine the room, i imagine the women
dressed in pale blues and pinks,

some without heads or arms—sitting
some without legs or waists—hovering
hundreds of flowering girls tucking spring into sleeves,
tucking and tugging at spring to stay alive

and so a shirtwaist for spring
a dress with a mannish collar, blousing over breast,
blousing over sweat, tapering to fit a female waist,
tapering to fit a female breath
sheer silk, cotton, linen
hand done pleats, hands done in by pleats
hands done in by darts and lace

colors of spring
pale blues, pale pinks, yellows, magentas, lavender, peach,

secret thoughts of spring
falling in love under a full moon, forever young
with money enough to buy a flower or two,
time enough to smell it
yes, from bareness to fullness a flower will bloom
anytime, every time spring enters a room
and here, near these machines, hundreds of flowering
girls

shirtwaist factory room 1911
crowded, hard, fast, too fast, closed windows,
locked doors, smell of piss, of sweat,
of wishes being cut to bits,
needle stabs, electric shocks, miscarriages over silk,
fading paisley, fading magenta,
falling in love will get you fired, forever old,
never fast enough, buying flowers is wasteful

so hurry, hurry, grind your teeth and soul
six dollars a week send to grandfather,
four dollars a week send to aunt ruth, sleep over the
machine and you're done for, way before you open your
eyes ma'm, madam, miss, mrs. mother, girlie
hundreds of flowering green spring girls in rows
waiting with needles in hands for spring to show

women workers
from ireland, poland, germany, france,
england, grenada, mississippi
thin clothes, thinner hopes, months full of why,
of how, of when
answers always less than their pay
but the sewing machines grew like weeds,
thick snake roots strangling the flowers every day
strangling the roses, daisies, lilies every day
hundreds of blooming girls
hundreds of blooming, spring girls

the shirtwaist building 1911
135 feet high, wooden, cold, three floors,
not enough stairs,
one fire escape ending in mid-air,
ending in the spring mid-air
a tender room of hundreds of blooming bright girls
hundreds of daisy bud girls who pray for spring
to enter their world,
who pray and sweat for spring to enter their world

the strike the year before
and they shouted; open the doors,
unwire the windows, more air,

more stairs, more quiet time, more fire escapes
and to the ground damn you,
and more toilets, more time to be sick,
more time to be well,
and remove the fear and slow it down,
for god's sake, slow it all, time, it's spring

they shouted
hundreds of flowering girls,
hundreds of flowering girls shouted
for spring to hurry, hurry and enter their world

and
triangle won a half day
but the doors remained locked,
windows remained wired, no extra air,
no extra quiet time, or sick time, the fear stayed,
nothing slowed
and god watched hundreds of flowering girls twirl
hundreds of flowering girls willow and twirl

march 25th 1911 at triangle
a worker is expendable
a sewing needle is not
a worker is bendable
a sewing needle is not
a worker can be sent straight to hell
a sewing needle is heaven sent
and must be protected well
a sewing needle is the finger of god
and must be protected well
over hundreds of flowering girls,
hundreds of flowering sweet dandelion girls

march 25th, smoke

smoke, stopping the machines

run to wired windows, run to locked doors,

run to the one and only fire escape,

everyone run to the air

hundreds of flowering girls

smoke

stopping eyes, stopping hearts, stopping worlds

elevator move faster, elevator you are a machine

managed by a human being move faster, c'mon faster

carry all the flowering girls, carry all the sweet,

sweet orchid girls

fire

catching bouquets of girls in a corner, tall, long

stemmed lilies on fire in a corner,

from bloom to ashes in a corner, smell

them in the rain hundreds of tulips girls

on a window ledge

pliés for life, on a window ledge lovely, ribboned young

ladies on their tiptoes twirling, twirling

an arabesque for life

hundreds of flowering girls

smell them in the rain

hundreds of jasmine girls

the ladders were too short

the hoses were too short

the men holding the nets were not gods, only men

who were never trained to catch falling bodies, or

falling stars, or hundreds of flowering girls, hundreds
of carnation bud girls

and the girls
were girls not angels jumping,
not goddesses flying or hovering
they smashed, they broke into
large pieces, smell them in the rain

and the sidewalks
opened in shame to meet the flowering girls
the sidewalks opened in such horrible shame to cradle
the remains of violets
and the gutters
bled for hours, choking on bones, shoes, buttons,
ribbons, holy sewing needles
the gutters bled for hours all the colors of spring
the cool magenta of delicate spring

and the fire ate
the locked doors and the wired windows,
ate the fast machines
in their narrow rooms, ate the lace and hand done pleats,
the silk, the cotton, the linen,
the crisp six dollars a week, the
eternal buzz of someone else's dreams
nightmares and screams of quiet girls,
loud skull cracking noises from shy girls
smell them in the rain, the lilacs, daffodils
in the rain

spring, 78 years later
triangle is now part of a university, with offices

and polished intellect, arched unwired windows,
hydraulically controlled and unlocked doors,
air conditioning, swivel chairs, marble walls and fire
alarms

but oh, hundreds of flowering girls still roam
hundreds of blushing spring girls still roam
78 years later in the paint, in the chrome
in the swivel of the chairs
hundreds of blossoms twirling in the air
daring to descend if ever, oh ever the fire comes again

yes, like lead they will drop
if ever, oh ever the fire comes again
to hundreds of flowering girls
smell them in the rain, iris, peonies, magnolias,
bending for the rain

In World War II, Women Got to Work

by Betsy Kuhn

14

Have you ever asked your grandmother, or maybe your great-grandmother, what she did during World War II? Maybe she drove a cab, or maybe she joined the marines. Yes, the marines. Eighteen thousand women served in the U.S. Marine Corps Women's Reserve, and do you know what they sometimes used to buff the barracks floor? Kotex pads.

One woman worked as a gas station attendant, though at first she knew little about cars: she thought the dipstick for checking the oil was kept in the station! And poet Maya Angelou decided, at age fifteen, to become a streetcar conductorette. The streetcar company didn't much want to hire this young black woman, though. It took her three weeks of going every day to their office before finally she says, "I was hired as the first Negro on the San Francisco streetcars."[8]

That's the kind of time it was. As awful as the war was, the upheaval it brought created many positive changes in the United States. Among the most striking were the new opportunities that arose for all women to work.[9] Just a few years earlier, during the Depression, jobs had been so scarce that some companies refused to hire married women. The husband, they felt, should have the job.

---

8 From *I Know Why the Caged Bird Sings* by Maya Angelou (New York: Random House, 1970), p. 229.
9 The one exception was Japanese Americans, who were interned by the U.S. government for most of the war.

All that changed when Japan bombed the navy base at Pearl Harbor, Hawaii, on December 7, 1941. With President Franklin D. Roosevelt at the helm, the nation entered the war. Suddenly men were joining the service in droves, leaving their jobs behind. And who was left to do the work? Women. Six million women entered the workforce during the war. They were butchers and barbers, chemists and electricians. They played in orchestras that had hired only men before; they formed all-girl bands. They pulled on slacks and went to work in defense plants, helping to build so many airplanes, ships, and other war goods that these "Rosie the Riveters" deserve much of the credit for the Allies' victory.

Women served as army and navy nurses, often near the fighting in far-flung corners of the world. Hundreds of thousands more "freed a man to fight" by joining new all-female branches of the military. They handled essential noncombat jobs in the Women's Army Corps (WAACs/WACs), Navy Women's Reserve (WAVES), Marines Corps Women's Reserve (WRs), and the Coast Guard (SPARs), doing everything from clerical work to driving trucks.[10] The Women Airforce Service Pilots (WASPs) flew military aircraft within the United States.

And some wives whose husbands had left for war simply learned how to manage the household on their own. All in all, women began to sense what they were capable of doing if given the chance; they saw new places and glimpsed new possibilities for their lives. And many were able to change their lives for the better.

10 WAAC was the acronym for the original name, Women's Army Auxiliary Corps; WAVES stood for the Women Accepted for Volunteer Service; and SPARS came from the Coast Guard motto: SEMPER PARATUS—Always Ready.

In 1941, Bethena Moore was working in Louisiana at a "huge laundry at Camp Polk," she says. The laundry "did the soldiers' clothes, khaki pants, shirts, whatever." Back then, the South held limited opportunities for black women like Bethena, who was from a sharecropping family. Sure, there were plenty of jobs as maids or cooks for white families, but little skilled work. Under the Jim Crow laws, segregation was a way of life. Did that bother her? "I could not let that bother me," says Bethena.

Out West and up North, new defense industries were looking for workers and paying them well. A new (though poorly enforced) federal law forbid these industries from discriminating by race. "My husband came to California in 1943," Bethena explains, one of a half million blacks to leave the South in the 1940s for defense jobs. Then "he sent for me." After a four-day train ride, she arrived in Richmond, California, near San Francisco, and Kaiser Shipyards quickly hired her.

"I went to welding school for two weeks," she says, learning what was traditionally a man's job. After more training, she was certified to do the final welds on Liberty ships, often on the flagpole, a thin steel ladder that was the tallest part of the ship.

"You'd be so high up, you couldn't hardly do much looking down," she remembers. "You had to carry all the equipment. You had to take your line [like a hose] connected to the welding machine below, and you had to take your rods which you used for welding—all that hung on you. You had on your welding suit that's all leather. And you had to have your hood. That was quite a bit of weight."

Despite the dangerous work, she had no time for fear. Sailors' lives depended on perfect work.

Flo Jordan also left the South to do war work, but her destination was Washington, D.C. Flo had grown up in the little town of Roystan, Georgia, "on a block that was all our relatives," she recalls. There were lots of family parties because "somebody in that group was always having a birthday." And they didn't leave home, not if they didn't have to.

"I went to business school so I could get a job," says Flo, who is white. "Back then, you took anything you could get practically." She'd passed the civil service exam, but there were no openings in Georgia. There were lots of jobs in Washington, though, and when she was eighteen, the War Department offered her one. Knowing nothing about the position, "I came," she says. "It was exciting to me." Her family "wanted to be sure I ate a good breakfast. Those were my instructions." After the war, she planned to come home and marry her high school sweetheart.

Fresh off the train in Washington, Flo took a cab to a big receiving center for the many young women arriving daily. "You went in there and they gave you a list of rooms to rent. . . . And they gave you a map to show you how you got on the streetcar and where to get off."

At the War Department, she worked at a typewriter in a big room that "had twice as many people as should have been in there." In fact, one million women worked for the federal government during the war; crowding was common. Flo met "young girls from all over the eastern U.S.," Catholics,

e more WOMEN at work
the sooner we WIN!

WOMEN ARE NEEDED ALSO AS:

FARM WORKERS	WAITRESSES	TIMEKEEPERS	LAUNDRESSES
TYPISTS	BUS DRIVERS	ELEVATOR OPERATORS	TEACHERS
SALESPEOPLE	TAXI DRIVERS	MESSENGERS	CONDUCTORS
		— and in hundreds of other war jobs!	

SEE YOUR LOCAL U.S. EMPLOYMENT SERVICE

Jews, women from all different backgrounds, she says, "and they were just like me." And she was earning money. (She'd always wanted "a really nice suit," so she bought herself a black suit at Hecht's department store. "I just thought it was gorgeous.")

As the war went on, the need for women workers became quite desperate. "The more WOMEN at work, the sooner we WIN!" read one government poster. It didn't matter if they were single, married, or even mothers. First Lady Eleanor Roosevelt recognized that if mothers were going to work, they would need help with child care. At her urging, the federal government began sponsoring some of the first day-care centers.

So what happened to all these dedicated working women when the war ended in 1945? You'd like to think the country said, "You've done a marvelous job. Keep at it." Instead, it said, "Thanks. Now please go home."

This was fine with many women. "I was glad," says Bethena, who was laid off as Kaiser closed their shipyards one by one. "I wanted the boys to come home." Lots of women, however, wanted to keep their jobs. They had come to like their work and the sense of self-reliance and economic independence it brought.

As for the military women, most of them had joined the service to help in the war effort and willingly left. In fact, the female service branches were scheduled to disband. But some women had found a home in the military and wanted to stay. And the military realized how much it needed women.

In 1948, two things happened. First, the number of married working women began to increase for the first time since the war's end. Second, President Truman signed the Women's Armed Service Integration Act, which basically authorized women to serve, on a permanent basis, in every branch of the military except the Coast Guard.

Did the fact that so many women worked and served during the war bring on these changes? The answer is complicated. Let's just say it played a role.

As for Bethena and Flo, Bethena and her husband stayed in California. Flo married a nice serviceman whom she met in a taxi and has lived in the Washington area ever since. She and Bethena both worked after having children.

And now, about that great-grandmother of yours: go talk to her. Maybe she has a story, too.

Why Eleanor Roosevelt (1884-1962) Still Rules

by Kathleen Krull

15

It caught me by surprise. I was pulsing friends of various ages, and every conversation included some type of quiet question to me—"So she was gay, right?"

Thirty years after Eleanor Roosevelt's death, sexual orientation seemed an odd summation on someone who permanently influenced American history. We're talking about a woman who was the First Lady during twelve years teeming with tension (the Great Depression, World War II). She was the very first First Lady to have a public life and career, the one with ideas so far ahead of her time that we're still catching up.

This surge of Eleanor power is all the more startling because we're talking serious late bloomer. Young ER was shy, awkward, frightened of everything, prone to depression, the opposite of a fashion plate—indeed, a genuine ugly duckling with a voice that warbled uncontrollably into giggles. People called her "Granny" even as a child.

Upon marriage, she didn't have the name-change dilemma of most women—she was already a Roosevelt, part of the wealthy dynasty that included her uncle, former president Theodore Roosevelt, and her fifth cousin and eventual husband, Franklin D. Roosevelt. The easiest path would have been no path—lurking in the background, being pampered, and coasting along with her children (she had six—one died in infancy) and a huge household staff.

But suddenly, with FDR's rise in local and then national politics, ER was in a strange position . . . of greater and greater power. Once he was elected president, she saw her access to him as a gift she could not afford to waste. What to do with it?

She decided to fight. Many of her experiences had fostered an extraordinary compassion and sensitivity—personal heartbreaks, volunteer work in her teens with those less privileged than herself, touring the battle-fields and working with the Red Cross during World War I. After she became the First Lady, ER wanted to make America better, more fair, and she chose to act as a major adviser to the President, becoming his "eyes" and "ears." And because polio had him confined to a wheelchair, she even became his "legs," traveling constantly to gather information that would fuel the policies she thought would result in the greatest good for the greatest number.

After hiring a voice coach, she spoke dynamically in person and on the radio. She wrote a daily newspaper column and numerous books. She called weekly press conferences restricted to women reporters (as a way of forcing newspapers to hire some). She badgered her husband (almost to death, some say) about the issues on her agenda: peace, better treatment for women and minorities, education, giving aid to the needy.

As for young people, ER passionately urged them to keep their greatest gift—curiosity—alive. During the Depression she helped found the National Youth Administration, which gave thousands of students much-needed part-time work. She also selected children's books for the Junior Literary Guild and started a magazine called *Babies—Just Babies* that advocated respect for children.

Ultimately, ER morphed into a heavyweight champion of the oppressed, the poor, the underdog. Her all-time favorite word was *hope.*

ER was sixty when FDR died. "The story is over," she told reporters. Ha! Actually, she went from national to global prominence. After the horror of the Second World War—the death of 60 million people and unimaginable destruction—she believed that a new organization, the United Nations, was the world's best hope. She became one of the first American delegates to the UN, putting in eighteen-hour days as a diplomat. Her cause was now the welfare of the human race, and she never took another vacation.

> Ultimately, ER morphed into a heavyweight champion of the oppressed, the poor, the underdog. Her all-time favorite word was hope.

Probably her greatest accomplishment was spearheading the Universal Declaration of Human Rights in 1948. She dedicated a solid year to persuading all delegates (even from countries where human rights were unheard of) to sign a document that began, "All human beings are born free and equal. . . ." The moment was historic, especially given that tensions between nations couldn't have been any higher.

Another claim to fame was as champion of African Americans during an era when discrimination, even lynching, was still accepted. People will never stop talking about her angry resignation, in 1939, from the Daughters of the American Revolution after the group blocked a performance by singer Marian Anderson. When she began hosting a weekly TV show in 1960, she had Dr. Martin Luther King, Jr., as her first guest.

She donated her hefty speaker's fees to charities that helped women. After President John F. Kennedy put her in charge of the Commission on the Status of Women, she issued a report that galvanized the American feminist movement. Ending discrimination in employment, equal pay for equal work—these were revolutionary ideas to some people.

As idealistic as ER was, she was also a shrewd warrior who hated to lose. She knew how to pick her battles during a time when hostility to women with power was more rabid than it is today. It is almost hard to imagine how controversial she was. Again and again, she was voted "the world's most admired woman" and "one of the most powerful people in Washington." At the same time she was the butt of nasty "Eleanor jokes." Some newspapers called for her to exit public life; some religious leaders blasted her actions as "unworthy of an American mother." During her White House years, an estimated three out of ten letters to the President were death threats or other hate mail about ER. The FBI saw her as such a threat to American society that it followed her everywhere and compiled a file of more than three thousand pages.

Others were won over by her magical balancing act of integrity, graciousness, and sincerity. Few people were so down-to-earth, with such a gift for putting people at ease. Her own life story was legendary for its change and growth. It inspired millions, especially women, who saw her doing things no woman had done before. "She gave off light," one friend said simply.

ER died at seventy-eight, after a stroke. A speaker at her funeral mourned, "What other single human being has touched and transformed the existence of so many?"

Except perhaps for her clothes, nothing about ER has gone out of date. She fought battles that are still being fought—the world is still not at peace.

Former First Lady turned New York senator Hillary Rodham Clinton has looked to ER as her role model. After revealing that she has gone so far as to imagine what advice ER might give, Clinton said, "I believe the world, and particularly our country, would be better off if we all spent a little time talking with Mrs. Roosevelt and less time yelling at each other."

Historians still argue about whether or not ER was gay. But by now, few of them will dispute her status as one of the greatest women who ever lived.

"No one can make you feel inferior without your consent."

AS A YOUNG WOMAN: "I took it for granted that men were superior creatures."

LATER IN HER CAREER: "As a rule, women know not only what men know, but much that men will never know."

"The ability to think for myself did not develop until I was well on in life and therefore no real personality developed in my youth."

"I have never been bored."

"Having learned to stare down fear, I long ago reached the point where there is no living person whom I fear, and few challenges that I am not willing to face."

"To be a citizen in a democracy, a human being must be given a healthy start."

"Hate and force cannot be in just a part of the world without having an effect on the rest of it."

"It's better to light a candle than to curse the darkness."

"The future belongs to those who believe in the beauty of their dreams."

—Eleanor Roosevelt

THE "REPRESENTING"

by Elisabeth Griffith

WHAT IS CONGRESS?

Imagine if girls were not allowed to run for student council or campaign to be president or treasurer of a club. Imagine if girls were allowed to be members of an organization and to attend its meetings but not allowed to speak for themselves, not allowed to "represent."

For most of American history, women were excluded from voting or running for office, which means that for most of American history, men were doing all the representing for women. But with the march of time, we have seen that all women have been empowered as some women represent.

American women have only been voting nationally since 1920, when the Nineteenth Amendment was ratified. Before 1776, a few white property-owning women in the North voted, but they lost that privilege following the Revolution. During the seventy-two-year campaign to win woman suffrage, from 1848 to 1920, fourteen states gave women the vote. Most were located west of the Mississippi River, where women's contributions to the frontier settlements were valued.

Women campaigned for the vote because they wanted to have their views heard and to speak for themselves on school boards and town councils, in state legislatures, and in Congress. Each step in women's slow progress in these forums was marked by a brave woman who risked being first.

Among the most important "firsts" in the political arena are those who threw their hats into the ring for a seat in the U.S. Congress, either in the House of Representatives or the Senate. Women want to help make laws for the whole country.

Congress is one of the three branches of the federal government, sharing a "balance of power" with the executive (the president) and the judiciary (the Supreme Court). Congress has two assemblies. The House of Representatives divides its 435 seats among states based on population measured by the census. The Senate gives states two votes each, for a total of 100. Puerto Rico, Guam, and the District of Columbia have non-voting delegates.

The Constitution assigns the Senate and House equal responsibility for declaring war, maintaining the armed forces, assessing taxes, borrowing money, minting currency, regulating commerce, and making all laws necessary for the operation of the government. The Senate holds exclusive authority to advise and consent on treaties and nominations, impeach the president, and confirm Supreme Court nominees.

16

Most of the congressional firsts have unique stories behind their government careers. In 1866, roughly fifty years before women could vote nationally, Elizabeth Cady Stanton, who launched the women's suffrage movement at Seneca Falls in 1848, was the first woman to run for Congress, from New York City's 8th district in Manhattan. She ran to protest women's exclusion from the Fifteenth Amendment, which gave black men—but not women—the right to vote. A century later, that same seat would be held by the formidable Bella Abzug, granddaughter of Orthodox Jews from Russia. Mrs. Abzug (a lawyer), elected in 1970, described herself as "impatient, impetuous, uppity, brash, and overbearing." In an era in which new members of Congress and women were expected to be seen and not heard, "Battling Bella" introduced her first bill on the opening day of her first session, demanding withdrawal of American troops from Vietnam.

Just as undaunted as Bella Abzug was the first woman ever elected to Congress, Republican Jeannette Rankin from Montana. An early college graduate with a degree in biology, Rankin won in 1916 (four years before women had national suffrage). She served two single terms (1917–19 and 1941–43) and both times cast the only votes against U.S. entry into world war. She is one of only a few women represented in the U.S. Capitol's

Statuary Hall, a collection of 97 statues (as of 2001) donated by individual states in tribute to notable citizens.

In 1932, Democrat Hattie Caraway from Arkansas was the first woman elected to the U.S. Senate "in her own right." Many of the women who have served in the Senate were widows of incumbents who had been appointed to fill their husbands' seats until an election could be held. When Senator Thaddeus Caraway died in 1931, his wife became one of those seat-warming widows, but went on to surprise political bosses when she literally threw her hat into the well of the Senate to declare her candidacy. Given the power of a Democratic nomination in the one-party South, she was elected without making one campaign appearance. Caraway, an early supporter of the Equal Rights Amendment, which had been introduced in 1923, was reelected in 1938. Having made the difficult transition from homemaker to Senate member, Mrs. Caraway sat knitting, listening, and learning. Taken under the wing of her flamboyant seatmate, Huey Long, she became an effective campaigner. She lost her seat to William Fulbright in 1944, when wartime restrictions on train travel kept her in Washington and away from her constituents in Arkansas.

HATS OFF?

> *"Throw one's hat in the ring.* Also, *toss one's hat in the ring.* **Announce one's candidacy or enter a contest. . . . This term comes from boxing, where throwing a hat in the ring formerly indicated a challenge; today the idiom nearly always refers to a political candidacy. [c. 1900]"**
>
> —*The American Heritage Dictionary of Idioms*

Only a few women have served in both the House and the Senate. The first and most famous was Margaret Chase Smith (Republican, Maine), also a congressional widow who succeeded her husband to the House, where she had served as his secretary. Mrs. Smith served four terms in the House (1940–48) and four in the Senate (1948–72), most of that time as the only woman senator. In an era of absenteeism where almost a quarter of the

Senate might fail to appear, Mrs. Smith held the all-time consecutive roll-call voting record (2,941 votes). Independent and stubborn, she voted for the nation more than her party or her home state. She was reserved but not reticent. She spoke up against the demagoguery of Senator Joe McCarthy when he hunted for alleged communists in Hollywood and the State Department in the 1950s. In the 1970s, she supported America's fighting the Vietnam War, an increasingly unpopular position.

Female firsts continue in today's House and Senate. In November 2000, Americans elected the largest number of women ever to serve in the Congress: 61 representatives (43 Democrats and 18 Republicans) and 13 senators (10 Democrats and 3 Republicans), for a total of 74. Among them were the first woman veteran elected to Congress, Representative Heather Wilson (Republican, New Mexico), and the first First Lady to run for office, Senator Hillary Rodham Clinton (Democrat, New York).

Between Jeannette Rankin and Hillary Rodham Clinton were other "first ladies." Shirley Chisholm (Democrat, New York) was the first African American woman to serve in Congress (1968–82) and in 1972 became the first Democratic woman to run for president. Patsy Mink (Democrat, Hawaii) was the first Asian American woman elected to Congress, having served in Hawaii's territorial government. In 2001, among women incumbents there were twelve African Americans, six Hispanics, and one Asian American, the highest number of women of color to date.

Women members of Congress report they have more constituents than just the voters in their districts. They become icons and receive mail asking for assistance from women all over the country. While these officeholders span the political spectrum from liberal to conservative, left to right, research concludes that no matter their party affiliation, they are more likely to cross party lines to support "women's issues" than are men. For example, voting records show that women in both parties worked together to fund breast cancer research, child-care programs, and equal pay for women. No matter what their party affiliation, having women in the committee room, at the table, changes the nature of the dialogue and the outcome of the debate.

Equally important, women in Congress inspire other women to join the "representing" by, for example, running for a seat on the school board, city council, or state legislature. And it's quite possible that the women who decide to act locally will one day decide to follow in the footsteps of Jeannette Rankin, Shirley Chisholm, Patsy Mink, and Hillary Rodham Clinton—throwing their hats in the ring for a seat in the highest legislative body in the land, the U.S. Congress. Although many public roles can lead to the presidency, it is quite possible that it will be from the ranks of congressional women that the first woman president will come.

17

LIFE IS SOMETIMES A
Fashion Parade

written and illustrated by Ilene Beckerman

From Eve's fig leaf to Cinderella's slipper, from the buttoned-up look of the Puritans to the mini-skirts of the 1960s, clothes have always been important as a mirror of the times, politically, socially, and economically. Historically, clothes were often used to create an image of women that society wanted them to fit, and now and again, women's clothing reflected the desire to break out of that mold. Women's clothing, much more so than men's, have been tangible examples of what's happening in the culture. Some of the styles we've worn in America have been practical, others ridiculous, most, somewhere in between. Take a look (and don't forget that what you wear makes a powerful statement about who you are and who you want to be).

1740s: The Perfect Puritan Woman

Puritans forbade fun—one look at their clothing tells you that. No frills. No color. How would you like to wear only black, gray, and brown? No Lycra bike shorts. No shorts! Just itchy wool! A white collar and white apron with every outfit, as a symbol of purity. Accessories: felt hat, woolen stockings, leather shoes. You can bet you won't find this outfit at the mall.

1780s: *An Elegant Colonial Lady*

How the times change fashion! Life was easier for some, and many women could afford to look prettier. Large bonnets, two or three kerchiefs worn together (was that the start of the layered look?). Petticoats, shirring, ribbons. Possible accessories: a locket or miniature portrait on a black cord, and a parasol. I think I saw Gwyneth Paltrow wear something like that in a movie.

1820s: *Enter the Empire Look*

A very high waistline and dainty puffed sleeves. Dig the white lace shawl, one of the first accessories made by machine. You'd never go out without your pantaloons. Pale blue shoes decorated with jewels tie around your ankles. And that white satin purse, decorated with amber beads—don't you love it?

1860s: *Scarlett O'Hara Takes Center Stage*

Here comes the Victorian look. Fuller figures, yeah! But a corset that squeezes you into an eighteen-inch waist, forget about it! I love the crinolines and those hoop skirts, but they're not great for jogging! But women in those days weren't expected to lead active lives. Just moving around the house must have been difficult enough. (Don't forget about Amelia Bloomer, though, who started wearing "bloomers," or trousers, in the 1850s—it took a while for that trend to catch on.) In the 1870s, you'd have to wear a bustle. Who wants a steel frame tied to your waist to make you have an enormous bottom?

1900s: The Gibson Girl Enters the Scene

Miles of hair piled in a pompadour on top of your head, a starched white blouse with a dark blue or black ascot scarf, a black broadcloth skirt, and a sailor hat—made famous by the artist Charles Dana Gibson. I could see myself looking like that. What about you?

1920s: The Flappers' Boyish Look Takes Over

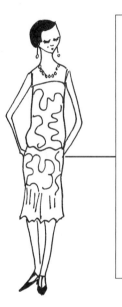

Cut your hair, flatten your bosom, ignore your waist, and show your knees . . . but be prepared for what your mother will say! The First World War ended and so did the restrictions on how women dressed. The Jazz Age had arrived, Gabrielle "Coco" Chanel, the first modern dressmaker, used jersey for the first time, women got the vote, and the world was never the same. Thank goodness.

1930s: A Feminine Revival

Subtle curves, graceful lines, and movie star glamour. Fashion closely follows the shape of the figure—clothes flowed. Necklines draped, backs were bare. The movies dramatized the new designs: think Ginger Rogers's dancing dresses, Greta Garbo, Jean Harlow. Furs were important. So was makeup. There was no "natural look."

1940s: Slacks Come of Age

World War II, and women enter the workforce. There you are working in a defense plant on an assembly line for the war effort. You're wearing slacks, the most practical clothing for work. Silk stockings are scarce, so you'll have to use leg makeup to tan your legs. And use an eyebrow pencil to draw a make-believe seam down your leg.

1947: The New Look

Haute couture, French custom-made clothes, is a big deal now. For women who can afford them, that is. The war is over and there's a new interest in fashion. Cloth is no longer rationed, so skirts are longer and fuller. The French designer Dior introduced "the New Look"—rounded bosom, small waist, and lots of glamour. You look feminine again with your hat and high-heeled shoes.

1950s: Mass-Produced Clothes

Now ready-to-wear becomes the big deal. Clothes are now made in factories, cheaply, so styles start to change quickly. One day you'll be wearing a straight shift or "sack," the next day the Trapeze look. Nylon stockings make big news.

1955: Teenage Power—You've Finally Arrived and Are Here to Stay

Whether you're swooning over Frank Sinatra or just having a Cherry Coke at the corner drug store, you'll probably be wearing a sweater set, circle skirt, bobby sox, and saddle shoes. The poodle skirt is soon to come. Everybody's starting to wear jeans everywhere except to bed.

1960: To What Lengths Does Fashion Go?

The mini-skirt, the micro-mini, the midi, or the maxi? Whichever you wear today, you'll wear the other tomorrow. You try to dress like President Kennedy's wife, Jacqueline, with her pared-down classic clothes, pillbox hats, and bouffant hair. Better throw out your print dresses, they're passé.

1962: The Audrey Hepburn Look Takes Over

Here comes the "Little Black Dress," long strands of pearls, big sunglasses, hair in a French roll. The Audrey Hepburn style arrives and never leaves. Half the population of the United States is now under twenty-five. You have disposable income and can buy those white go-go boots Nancy Sinatra later sang about.

1968: The Hippies Make the Scene

Enter unisex dressing, tie-dye, love beads, bell-bottoms, flower-power prints, flower children, and the granny look. My, what would the Puritans say about the cutout clothes, see-through inserts of sheer fabric, see-through midriffs, and all that jewelry?

1970s: Goodbye, Glamour, Hello, Happy Days

Women go to work. Separates and sportswear are hot. Polyester enters the scene—ugh! The bikini and the string bathing suit make big news for such little fabric. Say hello to disco— leotards, wrap skirts, hot pants, spandex, psychedelic colors . . . and John Travolta in *Saturday Night Fever*.

1980s: *Anything Goes*

Influenced by MTV, anybody can wear anything anyplace. Fashion magazines become bibles. Patches go with jeans. Sneakers go wild. Punks go crazy with their anti-fashion fashion: safety pins, Mohawk dos, pierced everything, black outfits, buckles, leather, and chains. Madonna goes provocative. Soap operas like *Dynasty* go for big shoulder pads. Princess Diana gets married in a fairy-tale dress. Talk about confusing fashions!

1990s: *Logos Are Everywhere*

Shopping becomes a form of recreation and entertainment. Designer names are everywhere, from jeans to pocketbooks. You can't walk down a street without seeing women dressed in clothes you have to read: DKNY, Chanel, Gucci. You are who you wear, but personally, I like my own name.

2000: *The Future of Fashion*

Women have been covered and uncovered, corseted and flattened. Bustled and bound. Pierced and tattooed. The twentieth century has been the most fashion-conscious so far. What does the twenty-first century hold in store besides fashion on the Web? Space-age clothes that make music and glow? Your guess is as good as mine. I'd sure like to see what's in *your* closet in 2040.

18

The Ladies' Pages

by Norma Johnston

Before the telephone, before TV, computers, e-mail, and the World Wide Web, there were women's magazines, and they were a hard-copy Internet for generations of girls and women. The only difference was that they were *periodicals* rather than *instant* reading.

First came the printing press and movable type, and they made newspapers possible. Now news could travel quickly and lead to evolution—or revolution. Newspapers in Colonial America often included, in addition to current events, information about clothing worn at the royal courts of Europe and notices of shipments of silks just arrived in Boston or New York along with "fashion dollies" clothed by European dressmakers to show seamstresses in the colonies the latest styles.

The next stage of evolution that happened for the ladies was the "Ladies' Column" or "Ladies' Page" in newspapers, which could fill empty space and sell more papers. Around the same time, printers began publishing *Lady's Annual* pocketbooks (so called because they fit easily into a lady's pocket) and marketing them as appropriate New Year's gifts. Containing interesting scientific information as well as poetry, etiquette advice, perhaps a fashion plate, these filled the need for a useful and appropriate item a gentleman could give a lady. Out of the Ladies' Pages and the pocketbooks was born, in the early years of the nineteenth century, the women's magazine.

The *magazine* was a brand-new publishing process and, used in this context, a brand-new word. A *foreign* word: from Arabic *makhazin* to Italian *magazzino* to French *magasin,* it meant a place where arms, ammunition, or supplies were stored. These new magazines were a storage place of valuable, useful, sometimes incendiary information and ideas for women and their daughters. By the middle of the nineteenth century, they were beginning to change the world.

Even more outrageously, they were largely being written, edited, and sold by girls and women!

Nearly everything a girl or woman wanted to know but didn't know whom, how, or where to ask (at least, not without getting into trouble) was in those magazines. The two most famous ones in the United States were *Godey's Lady's Book,* edited by the celebrated Sarah Josepha Hale, and *Peterson's Magazine.* During the next fifty to seventy-five years others followed: the *Ladies' Home Journal, Woman's Home Companion, McCall's,* and many more.

Here is some of what you could find in a women's magazine of the nineteenth century: ❖ short stories and serialized novels by well-known authors ❖ information on the latest styles and how to copy them at home ❖ poetry, songs, and essays ❖ scientific, medical, financial information ❖ how to start a home-based business ❖ "a piece of new fashionable music each month" ❖ advice to the lovelorn (and battered women) ❖ a page for pen pals' correspondence, with anonymity guaranteed ❖ how-to articles ❖ a children's page and/or page on children's fashions ❖ book reviews ❖ "receipts [recipes] for table, toilette, sickroom, etc." ❖ a classified ad column or section, plus small illustrated ads for almost anything a lady might want to buy (from corsets to furniture) ❖ opportunities for readers to make money

In 1862, subscriptions to *Peterson's Magazine* were "Two dollars a year, invariably in advance," and subscribers were promised nearly one thousand pages, including twenty-five to thirty colored fashion plates (now much prized by collectors), and around eight hundred black-and-white drawings (fashions; embroidery, knitting, and dressmaking patterns; story illustrations) per year. The content of *Godey's Lady's Book* was similar. So were the methods of producing the illustrations. The black-and-white ones (often including "a picture suitable for framing") were printed from woodcuts. The colored fashion plates were real works of art—steel engravings portrayed ladies (sometimes with children) in an idealized indoor or outdoor social setting; after these pages had been printed in black-and-white they were mailed to women artists who, working in their homes, hand-tinted the engravings with watercolor paints.

In the early 1890s came the first major changes in magazine publishing. One had to do with how the industry was financed. When *Peterson's Magazine* began in 1862, advertisements in magazines had been small in size. But publishing costs, and therefore subscription prices, had risen in the post–Civil War years. In 1893, several monthly magazines dropped their subscription and per-copy prices drastically (in order to attract thousands more readers) and began concentrating on making profits from sales of advertising space.

This soon led to the second major change, which is still evident today. Magazines began to be published for very specific reader categories (what is now called "market niches")—no longer just "general," "women," "children"—to which certain categories of advertising would appeal. For example, the "5¢ a copy" magazines were geared toward a poorer, more rural readership than the middle-class "10¢" ones, and carried ads for farm equipment and moderately priced household items, rather than the more high-style, higher-priced items that could be expected to appeal to city readers. Of course, especially in women's and children's magazines, there was a great deal of advertising and editorial content that would appeal to a very broad spectrum of readers.

Other changes also occurred in the 1890s, thanks to the influx of advertising money. Magazines such as the *Ladies' Home Journal* could be published in tabloid size (11 1/2" by 16 1/2") rather than the six by ten inches of *Peterson's Magazine.* The new women's magazines could take advantage of modern technology to produce magazines that were considerably livelier and more interesting-looking than in the past. They were also able to purchase rights to publish excerpts from the latest books by the most highly regarded writers. Because subscription prices dropped, more women could afford to subscribe.

Two wonderful opportunities for all women and girls were offered matter-of-factly by these women's magazines of one hundred years ago. One was that anyone could submit stories and articles for publication—age or race wasn't an issue because it wasn't known, and gender didn't matter. The other required no talent, only an outgoing personality and a desire to make money. Magazines needed subscribers because advertising rates were pegged to the size of the guaranteed readership. So readers were urged to "form a Subscription Club"— that is, to urge family, friends, and neighbors to order magazine subscriptions from them. The rewards were considerable, running to as high as a thousand dollars (in addition to the regular commission) to whoever recruited the most club members in a certain period of time. The magazines made clear that anyone living in the United States or Canada could become a "registered agent." It was a wonderful opportunity for young people.

These women's magazines treated their young readers with respect, taking for granted that they could earn money, grow a garden, even turn the family attic into a comfortable, stylish room for themselves with only a little professional help for the most major elements of carpentry.

One striking characteristic of magazines of the 1860s had been their absolute avoidance of any mention of the Civil War, probably because they had subscribers in both North and South, even though few issues could ever penetrate the blockade to reach Confederate subscribers. The attitude of publishers was quite different during World War I (1914–18); girls and women were rallied to war-relief projects. And during World War II (1941–45) there was no way for any publication, even for children, to avoid acknowledging that there were few households not affected by a father, uncle, brother, cousin, son in the midst of fighting, and often a mother, sister, daughter working in "war plant" factories. Food and gasoline were rationed; fashion was frozen (by the skimpy fabric yardage legally allowed). Magazines helped women and girls "keep the home fires burning" and their "chins up" by offering advice on how to "use up, wear out, make do, do without."

It was during World War II that another revolution came about: *Calling All Girls,* followed by *Seventeen.* These were teen magazines, specifically published for young women whose girlhood was spent worrying about World War II. While not as sophisticated as teens today, they were nowhere near as sheltered as their mothers' generation had been, and the magazines reflected this. They "told it like it was," and their fashion, dating, financial, and scientific recommendations at the time were the most cutting-edge information available—so much so that girls often hid the magazines from mothers, boyfriends, and, above all, brothers.

Best of all (or so it seemed to us would-be authors), they bought and published stories by teen readers. *Seventeen* held a yearly short-story contest; those stories still "hold up" today. Lois Duncan, now an internationally famous suspense writer, had her first short story published in *Senior Prom* when she was fifteen. I never had the courage to submit one of my stories to a magazine. But I cut stories out of *Seventeen* and *Calling All Girls,* out of *Ladies' Home Journal, Woman's Home Companion, Good Housekeeping,* and others. They helped me learn how to write.

When radio and movies came along, many people predicted that magazines (and newspapers and books) would soon be dead and buried. They said the same thing when TV, and now the Internet, came into millions of American homes. Magazines are still around and there's something for every kind of woman: magazines for a variety of ethnicities, political ideologies, and interests.

And do you know what? The sticky issues and situations that today's magazine readers encounter in their lives are, at their core, the same ones I . . . and my mother . . . and my grandmother, and her mother . . . ran into. If you don't believe me, just read between the lines of those old women's magazines! The social customs, values, and etiquette in them may now seem laughable—or in the case of medical/scientific/beauty advice, sometimes downright dangerous—but the principles behind them aren't. Things like valuing family . . . and helping those in need . . . judging people by their character, not their religion or ethnicity . . . having self-respect, and respecting others. Having integrity. Realizing that "the small ceremonies of daily life" are neither unimportant nor put-on phoniness, but a way of getting along with others better, and of sharing with them a gift of grace. Being proud to be a woman, and allowing others their pride, too. All of which was first "memorialized" in women's magazines.

P.S.: Even though some of today's magazines are under fire because of the values they appear to endorse, we must acknowledge that even they are part of the ongoing history of women's experience in America.

by Ophira Edut

Beauty Can

By the time I was snappin' on my first beige training bra,
I wanted to be beautiful so badly I could taste it.

Translation: I noticed that so-called traditional good looks
(which, as a chunky, funky Jewish girl, I didn't have) seemed
to hold more power than intelligence, creativity, imagination, and
personality (which I had aplenty). I thought that meant I should draw
attention to my appearance—by being physically "beautiful" in all the
ways that models and magazines mapped that out.

Although I didn't know it at the time, what I really wanted was to be
heard. Respected. Called on more in class. A chance to kick my sexist math
teacher where it counts when he mocked the girls as airheads and said we'd
be better off taking home economics than calculus.

So we girls got the message: "If you want people to listen to you,
they've gotta look at you first. So get to the mall and the Clinique counter,
honey—it's makeover time!"

Sure, I wanted to feel good about my body, but more than anything I
wanted to feel whole—like my insides and outsides weren't two separate
countries locked in a constant border dispute. But this separation of girls'
minds, bodies, and souls is encouraged everywhere. A recent *Vanity Fair*
magazine cover featuring a well-known actress trumpets: "A Beauty with
Brains, Too!"—as if this "phenomenon" were as rare and newsworthy as a
sighting of Elvis sitting at Burger King.

History has demanded these extremes from girls and women for centuries.
In the twentieth century, American women were offered more body-contorting
contraptions than an Olympic gymnast: corsets, scalp-searing hair relaxers,

Be a Beast

cellulite cream, skin bleach, thighmasters. Heck, I thought my little cream-colored A-cup was torturously snug about the armpits. Had I been born in the early 1900s, I would have passed out on the regular from waist-cinching corsets made of whalebone that mangled women's rib cages and sucked their waists down to an impossible "hourglass" shape.

I'm still waiting for the day that women's bodies aren't expected to fit the fad of the moment. But it's been happening for a *looong* time.

Example: Today, *Cosmopolitan* is probably the queen of all body angst–inspiring fashion magazines, right? Good luck finding any body fat in there. But back in 1910, the magazine was publishing *anti*-dieting articles. One doctor even wrote a column saying that women who weighed around 185 pounds were in great shape, and that most fat people were "vigorous, efficient, and successful people who lead happy, healthy, and useful lives."

Imagine how differently we'd feel about our bodies if *Cosmo* was still dishing out that advice today!

That's cuz back in the early 1900s, dieting was actually considered unhealthy and strange. Babies had a harder time surviving childbirth in those days, and people often died from contagious diseases. Most doctors spent their time whipping up vaccines, not miracle fat-busting formulas. In fact, any doc from that era would have told you that body fat was essential to fending off disease. If a fatal illness struck the town, an undernourished person could be the first to go.

Money also talks. Around that same time, a wealthy ex-businessman named Horace Fletcher promoted one of the earliest fad diets: chewing each bite of food until it had absolutely no flavor or texture left. *Yucccch.* But Fletcher had the cash to make himself heard, and his idea caught on for a few years.

With every war, every economic boom and bust, every political change, women's bodies have been expected to change accordingly. During World War I, when the economy slimmed down and food got scarce, magazines began to call fat "unpatriotic." Eating well was suddenly a crime, not a *mitzvah* (that's what we Jewish peeps like to call a good deed).

Another example: Shortly after the abolition of slavery, African American women were targeted with hair-straightening and skin-bleaching products, designed to "improve" their appearances. (Translation: to make them look whiter—believed to be a sign of an improved life.) This message has stuck around for more than a century. The media give black girls the message that long, straight locks (often easier to weave than achieve) are more "feminine" and attractive.

Not to sound like an *Unsolved Mysteries* commercial here, but it's almost a conspiracy. First the times change—okay, that's natural. Then the fashion industry and the magazines develop some out-there wardrobe concept and heave it on us, even though 99.9 percent of us couldn't wear it comfortably without donating half a rib cage to science. Meanwhile, some rich businessperson invests millions in a cockamamie wonder diet, and *boom*—suddenly half the country is following another crazy weight-loss fad. C'mon, people, aren't we supposed to be smarter than this?

Oddly, in spite of all these size-reducing gizmos and fads, Americans' weight has gone up steadily over the last hundred years or so. Girls today are developing earlier than a couple decades ago, and Americans are just bigger all around. It's not always due to good health, alas. Healthy food is still easier to get if you've got money, and many poor people in the United States are both overweight *and* malnourished.

So how do we make sense out of it all and figure out just how to love our bodies in the midst of the madness? I say we start by fighting for a world that makes room—permanently—for a range of body shapes, sizes, and colors. The answer is not to replace fat with thin, or thin with fat.

Let's recognize that there's a spectrum out there, and let's work to see that reflected in our own attitudes and in the media.

We could also stand to change some thinking that we learn from day one. "Fat" is not a synonym for "ugly." Neither is "dark" or "nappy" or "old," or whatever word we might substitute there.

Lastly, as I learned, looks are not a substitute for personality. Even if we only develop A-cup chests (not that there's anything wrong with that), developing A-plus minds will get us a lot farther in the long run. Trust me. We've gotta see the beauty in our whole selves. Sure, you may never go to prom with that hot guy from the varsity wrestling team (or you just might . . . you never know). But ten years later, when his high school charm is history and you're interviewing for the same job, or he's still making the same "dumb blonde" jokes, you'll put him in an intellectual headlock. *Boom.* Down in thirty seconds.

And, sisters, isn't that the kind of history we really want to make?

GIRL GROUPS MEAN

You know how it is. Something totally bad just happened—you saw the boy you like at the movies with another girl, or your teacher put you down in front of the whole class, or you got in a big screaming fight with your mom. What do you do? Get by yourself, put on your earphones, and listen to your favorite famous girl-friends singing just for you. Girl singers express feelings you can't always put into words. And it's not just the lyrics—they might not have even written those. The power lies in their voices, the way they capture what it's like to be furious, miserable, or just dreamy. Most of all, you appreciate the way they sound so free.

When I was in high school in Seattle, lots of boy rock-and-roll heroes made me swoon. But I got something different from the women artists I loved. Debbie Harry from Blondie was unbelievably beautiful, but in hits like "Hanging on the Telephone" she sounded as upset as I'd get over some jerk not calling back when he said he would. Chrissie Hynde of the Pretenders was supercool in her leather jacket and boots, and she nailed my own confusion about sex and independence in tender-tough songs like "Brass in Pocket." Chrissie helped me be a little braver as I worked behind the counter at my summer job selling German sausages at the Seattle Center amusement park, or as I stood in the back at the Gorilla Gardens all-ages club, wishing I had the guts to ask some lame punk boy to dance.

20

GIRL POWER

by Ann Powers

I loved my rock-music heroines so much that I just assumed they were the best girl singers who'd ever existed. But then at one all-ages show a local band covered this song, "Remember (Walkin' in the Sand)," by a group called the Shangri-Las. It told about a girl's heartbreak when her boyfriend moves away and betrays her. Boring story, but the song was so dramatic and the sound so wild that I went out and bought a Shangri-Las' record the next day.

I couldn't believe it. Here were these four sisters, Catholic schoolkids like me but from the early 1960s, before feminism (with a capital F), or hippies, or anything. Yet they wore leather pants, Beatle boots, and giant hairdos; they sang about sneaking out at night, dating guys who rode motorcycles, and dancing "real, real close." Their voices were high and sassy, with laughter fighting a big sob underneath. The best thing about their songs like "Leader of the Pack" and "Give Him a Great Big Kiss" was how the singers turned them into a lunchroom conversation, trading jokes and secrets and sealing them with a blown smackeroo.

I soon discovered other girl groups from the 1950s and 1960s to love. There were the Shirelles, high school pals from Passaic, New Jersey, who wrote a lot of their own songs, like "I Met Him on a Monday," which

THE SHANGRI-LAS

took off from a jump-rope rhyme. They also sang "Will You Love Me Tomorrow?" the best song ever about sex and self-respect.

There were the Ronettes, produced by the legendary Phil Spector, who was married to their lead singer, Ronnie. Everybody called him their Svengali, as if he totally controlled them; he had a cool way of making the mix sound really huge, like the Ronettes were singing in a tunnel. But what made songs like "Be My Baby" hit so hard was Ronnie's voice, as meltingly luscious as cotton candy, but all bittersweet inside.

Martha Reeves and the Vandellas were as hard-rocking as the Ronettes were seductive, connecting the girl-group sound to gospel and the blues. They were on the famous Motown label, from Detroit, along with the Supremes, who were like a supermodel girl group, so classy and flirty on songs like "Where Did Our Love Go?"

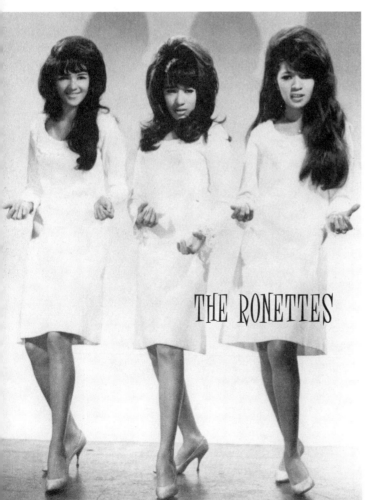

THE RONETTES

As much as I admired the women who'd stood alone in bands filled with boys, these girl groups offered something even better: sisterhood. The great thing about the girl groups was that they were about girls being together—gossiping, catfighting, making up, and supporting each other through the hardest times, as girlfriends do. By expressing the power young women found in each other, girl groups opened up a whole new view of what a "young lady" could be. She could be loud, have desires, and make mistakes, but still find joy in her own strength of heart.

Girls still fall in love and don't know what to do about it, find themselves betrayed by friends they thought would never do them wrong, and have to face hard choices, sometimes all alone and in secret. Girl groups address these troubles, and they also celebrate the excitement of being young and feeling like you're going to win what you want one fine day.

In the past, some snobby critics discounted the value of girl groups because most didn't write their own music, and it was just bubblegum for kids anyway. But feminism has taught us to appreciate everyday magic. And as far as writing their own material, first off, some of the most important songwriters of that time were young women. (Ellie Greenwich, who co-wrote "Out in the Street," an awesome song about loving a bad boy, and Carole King, whose credits include "Will You Love Me Tomorrow?," were songwriting stars.) And besides, the words and melodies only blossomed when the voices of young women brought them alive: using the power of rhythm and melody to dig out everyday emotions and make everybody hear how important they are—and by extension, how much every girl's passion, pain, and courage matters to the world.

In the early 1960s, everyone agreed that what girl groups had to say was both meaningful and totally fun. The Beatles even said that they hoped they sounded as good as the Ronettes. But once the boys took over the rock

MARTHA AND
THE VANDELLAS

133

THE SUPREMES

game, girl groups had it harder. A few succeeded—you probably know that awesome disco anthem, "We Are Family," from Sister Sledge—but mostly girls got pushed aside by guys waving their big guitars around.

Then punk exploded in the late 1970s; this rough and bratty underground music that mostly stayed underground had a big effect. Punk helped girls realize that they could play noisy rock, too. The Runaways, from Los Angeles, was a proto-punk band and one of the first all-girl bands. Joan Jett, Lita Ford, and their bandmates were like the Shangri-Las as mall rats in rainbow jeans. If *they* could play so hard and loud, a lot of girls thought, why couldn't we?

A few years later came the Go-Go's and the Bangles, the first all-girl bands to have really major hits. These band started out in Hollywood like the Runaways, dressed in crazy vintage clothes, and sang about ruling the scene together ("We Got the Beat," by the Go-Go's) and about falling in love one by one ("Eternal Flame," by the Bangles). It was just like the golden days of the Shirelles, except these bands played all their instruments, too.

Tons of girl bands came up through punk. Most stayed basically unknown. In the early 1990s, another bunch caught the public's ear, with the feminist metal chicks in L7 and the brilliant political punks in Bikini Kill and Bratmobile making girl music tougher and more confrontational. All of this history happened before the Spice Girls, who mixed up every era in their mainstream version of girl power. "If you wanna be my lover, you gotta get with my friends," they sang as they jumped around in their first video like a cheerleading squad on a rampage. They brought back that feeling of strength in numbers that the girl groups always had. And they haven't been alone. TLC and Destiny's Child both update girl-group style for the hip-hop era. They're super sexy and sly, ready to take down any guy who gives them grief. The Dixie Chicks and SheDaisy send the same message in country music, while Kittie and the Donnas play hard and fast, just like the Runaways did.

You could even say we're in a girl-group renaissance. At least it sounds that way sometimes, as the radio vibrates with the sounds of these young artists giving new form to the emotions girls have shared at least since the invention of the telephone, and probably much longer. One thing's for sure, though: there's always room for more women making songs together.

So grab your real best friends, raise your voices, and soon you could be the leader of your own musical pack.

THE GO-GO'S

January 2001

Dear Nadine, Eliza, and Marina,

You are making history. That's what I think when I see you in practice, or at your races. There you are, so young and yet already training as serious athletes, preparing to race your fastest times ever. What would your great-grandmother Ella think? Oh, I imagine she would envy your sleek team suits and your smooth strokes. She would marvel at the rigor of your practices and the drama of your meets. She would be impressed that you train side by side with boys. Let's face it: Ella would envy all you girls growing up in the United States in the twenty-first century!

What has been the history of women in sports in the United States? Well, for a long time the story was slim to none. Sports were thought too rough for women: girls might get hurt, but even worse, their expenditure of energy in sport might reduce the available energy for procreation. Very limited recreational activity was the norm for girls and women until well into the twentieth century. These limitations explain the experience of someone like your great-grandmother, Ella, who loved baseball and who was very capable, but who could not imagine being on a team. If she shed her apron and whacked the ball over the backyard fence, it was something of a darling family joke. She wasn't an athlete stepping up to the plate for her team. Even powerhouse Ella couldn't imagine that for herself.

Now, there were always brilliant exceptions to that rule. For example, the suffragist Annie Smith Peck surmounted the ideas about female weakness with heroic demonstrations of strength and endurance. In 1895, she climbed the Matterhorn in the Swiss Alps; in 1897, she reached the summit of Mount Orizaba in Mexico; and in 1911, upon

by Fritz Beshar

THE PLAYING FIELD

reaching the summit of Mount Coropuna in Peru, she unfurled a banner inscribed "Votes for Women." In 1934, Babe Didrikson pitched a full inning for the Philadelphia Athletics against the Brooklyn Dodgers. In 1952, Andrea Mead Lawrence won two gold medals in the first women's slalom events at the Olympics. In the 1960s, tennis superstar Billie Jean King set the women's record for holding the most Wimbledon titles; later, she set the record straight when she soundly defeated Bobby Riggs in "the battle of the sexes."

But remember: the achievements of these girls and women were the exception, not the rule. Even after some women had demonstrated remarkable prowess as athletes, girls and women were not given full opportunity to train and compete. Why not? There continued to be concerns that sports were damaging to a girl's body: some thought their bodies were too fragile; others thought displays of the female body in sport improper. Even in the late 1960s, I was cautioned that if I didn't "watch out," I would develop "big muscles" and then I would "never be thin enough."

Then came a revolution in the law in

BILLIE JEAN KING

1972. That was the moment in history you need to know about. This was the beginning of Title IX.

Title IX is a section of the Civil Rights Act of 1972, the set of laws enacted as a tribute to Martin Luther King, Jr.'s dream of equality under law for all citizens. The Act guarantees equal rights in a number of arenas: employment, housing, voter registration, and education. Title IX is the section of the law devoted to equality in education. Title IX prohibits discrimination in all educational activities that receive federal money, including athletics and physical education. Under Title IX, the per capita expenditure for boys' and girls' sports must be the same.

Under Title IX, schools have been forced to greatly increase their sports programs for girls to match those of the boys. Sometimes it took courageous and outrageous women to force schools to live up to their requirements under the law. For example, on March 3, 1976, Chris Ernst, captain of the outstanding Yale Women's Crew, led her teammates into the office of the athletic director, where they stripped to the waist to reveal "Title IX"— written in bold black marker—on their backs and chests. Chris then read a statement protesting the lack of a locker room for the women athletes, while a stringer from the *New York Times,* alerted by the team, clicked photos of those powerful backs inscribed with "Title IX." The *Times* ran the story the next day, provoking an intense response—including donations for new showers. Chris was my coach the next year when I began rowing at Yale, and she inspired all of us to work harder than we ever imagined we could. One of the rowers who used the new showers with me was my childhood friend Ginny Gilder, who rowed at Yale and went on to win a silver medal at the 1984 Olympics. Just last year, Ginny and her father donated a new boathouse to Yale. You can be sure Ginny made sure the new Yale boathouse has plenty of room for the women rowers!

The spending requirements under Title IX have brought huge changes in the culture of schools, and in girls' interest in sports. Before the enactment of Title IX, in 1971, only one in twenty-seven high school girls played sports. In the year 2000, one in three high school girls played sports in school. And the involvement of girls in organized sports programs has changed the face of girls' and women's sports all around the country because so many girls who develop the habit of intense exercise as children continue to be athletic.

The elementary school programs produce high school athletes. And where do those budding high school athletes go? Some go on to college, where Title IX insists women's sports be funded on a par with men's sports. Some go on to train for higher and higher goals, including professional sports, national competitions, and even the Olympics. In the 1972 Olympics there were 43 events for women and less than 15 percent of the athletes were female. In the 2000 Olympics, 42 percent of the athletes were women and there were 121 events for those female athletes. As the field of competition widens, the more reason for more women athletes to keep training to higher and higher levels. And the more training, the more success, and thus the greater women's participation and achievement in an array of sports. And when you're successful? Well, then everyone wants to be part of your story. So now there are more girls and women involved in sports, and more money in professional women's sports and sponsorships for women athletes. In response, the girls and women keep getting better and better in their sports, and coming closer and closer to the standards set by male athletes.

That's where you come in, you girls of the twenty-first century. Under Title IX you have the right to be supported in your athletic efforts to the same degree as boys. With the progress Title IX has brought to girls' sports, you have more and more training opportunities, and more and more accomplished female athletes to look up to. Want to be the next Jenny Thompson, with gold medals strung from your neck? Go for it. Women athletes, for centuries, have been looking forward to your opportunity to make yourself the best. The law supports you, and so does recent history. You're only getting better!

And so, Nadine, Eliza, and Marina, keep going to practice, keep racing for the team, keep swimming across the wide water of your dreams with your highest aspirations in mind. All of us in the stands watching you and your fellow athletes appreciate that you are part of the new story that equal rights for women under the law has allowed to take shape. Any girl—athlete or friend of an athlete, competitor or fan—can appreciate that story!

Love,
Mom

22

I will never forget the speech that Julie Croteau gave in Clearwater Beach, Florida, on October 26, 1991. At the time, Croteau was a twenty-year-old student who'd succeeded in becoming the first woman to play on a men's college varsity baseball team. She was also an extra in the movie <u>A League of Their Own</u>, and she'd come to Florida to speak about her experiences to the players of the All-American Girls Professional Baseball League, who'd inspired the film. As she looked out at more than one hundred women from the league, she fought to control her emotions.

Who Was First, an

"I've been playing baseball since I was five," she said. "I've had some of the best experiences of my life on that diamond. I've also had some of the worst. . . . I've been spit on, called derogatory names, been locked out and been locked in, felt isolated and alone, and been harassed. I've been cut from teams I deserved to be on. I've even been called the team slut. All for the love of a children's game."

Croteau went on to ask the other pioneering athletes in the room to do what they could to help more girls play baseball. When she was through, the older women embraced her with their applause and their hugs. They understood her struggles because they, too, had risked ridicule and worse to play the game they loved—in the first women's professional baseball league. "We were going against society, with its rules and regulations telling us that this is the way we should grow up and this is what we should do," remembered All-American catcher Shirley Stovroff. "And therefore, we did take a beating."

Croteau's speech stayed with me because it chronicled so dramatically the costs of being first. Imagine working so hard that against all odds you achieve your goal, only to be taunted or attacked by closed-minded people who have decided you don't belong. But Croteau also showed me the rewards of being first. Her grace under pressure during her first public speech was a direct result of the self-confidence and determination she'd developed over years of sticking her neck out.

History is full of women who stuck their necks out, heroic women

Why It Matters
by Sue Macy

who braved isolation or ridicule to be the first females in their fields. Here are just a few.

Jerrie Cobb (1931–)
First Female Astronaut Candidate

Jerrie Cobb earned her pilot's license when she was sixteen years old, but that was just the beginning. In 1959, this Oklahoma native was recruited to undergo a secret battery of physical and psychological tests given to potential U.S. astronauts. Dubbed "the first astronautrix" by *Time* magazine, Cobb passed all of the tests with flying colors. But after twelve additional women qualified for astronaut training, the National Aeronautics and Space Administration (NASA) suddenly canceled the women's program.

Congressional hearings followed, and some members of the House

Space and Astronautics Committee felt that the United States should continue to compete with the Soviet Union to launch the first woman into space. NASA rejected the idea, however, and in 1963 the Soviets won that aspect of the space race when they sent Valentina Tereshkova up for a three-day flight. It would be twenty years before the first American woman, Sally Ride, would leave the earth's orbit. In the meantime, Jerrie Cobb left the country in 1964, moving to South America to do missionary work among the indigenous people in remote portions of the Amazon. But she still yearned to travel in space, even as a senior citizen. "Nothing means more to me," she told a reporter in 1998. "This is something I would give my life for."

Jeannette Rankin (1880–1973)
First U.S. Congresswoman

Jeannette Rankin spent her life fighting for two main causes: women's rights and peace. This native of Missoula, Montana, led the campaign that compelled the Montana legislature to give women the vote in 1914, several years before that right was granted by the federal government. Two years later, she ran for the U.S. House of Representatives on the Republican ticket and won, taking her place as the first woman ever elected to either the House or the Senate. In Washington, she helped draft a constitutional amendment granting the vote to women nationwide. Although the amendment stalled in the Senate, women did finally win the vote in 1920.

During her term in Congress, Rankin spoke passionately against the entry of the United States into World War I and was defeated upon her bid for reelection. Trained as a social worker,

Rankin stayed in Washington to lobby for women's and pacifist causes until 1940, when she was elected to Congress again. This time the nation was voting to enter World War II, and Rankin cast the only "no" vote. "Few members of Congress have ever stood more alone while being true to a higher honor and loyalty," future president John F. Kennedy would say. Jeannette Rankin left Congress in 1943, but she campaigned for peace for the rest of her life. In 1968, when she was eighty-seven years old, she led five thousand women in a march on Washington against the Vietnam War.

Maggie Lena Walker (1867–1934)
First Female Bank Founder and Bank President

Born in Richmond, Virginia, just after the Civil War, Maggie Lena Mitchell Walker was the daughter of a former slave and a man who had been an abolitionist. When Walker was growing up, she joined the Grand United Order of St. Luke, an African American organization that provided health care and burial arrangements for its members. Walker stayed active in the order as she continued her education, becoming a teacher and a part-time insurance agent and studying bookkeeping at night. She developed a reputation as a dynamic speaker with business savvy, who often encouraged children to save their money.

Walker thought she could strengthen her community by opening a bank owned and operated by African Americans, using the money deposited there to finance homes and businesses. On November 2, 1903, she achieved her dream, founding the St. Luke Penny Savings Bank. Maggie Walker served as president of the bank until 1930, when St. Luke merged with two other African American banks to become the Consolidated Bank and Trust Company. She became chairperson of the board of directors of the Consolidated and held that title until her death. The bank is still operating in Virginia today.

Dr. Mary Edwards Walker (1832–1920)
First Woman Awarded the Congressional Medal of Honor

Mary Edwards Walker was ahead of her time in a number of ways. Born in Oswego, New York, Walker was an early proponent of women's rights. She attended New York's Syracuse Medical College and graduated in 1855 to become one of only a small number of female doctors in the United States. She also married fellow student Albert Miller that year, but wore trousers at her wedding instead of a dress and refused to promise to "obey" him in her wedding vows or to change her last name to his.

When the Civil War broke out, Walker headed to Washington, D.C., with plans to join the medical corps. At first she was allowed to work only as a volunteer, but after two years she was commissioned as an assistant surgeon. Walker's work often took her behind Confederate lines, and in 1864 she was captured and held in jail for four months. After the war, President Andrew Johnson presented her with the Congressional Medal of Honor for her bravery and sacrifice. Although the medal was one of nine hundred revoked in 1917 for lack of war documentation, Mary Walker refused to give it back and wore it until she died. The honor was restored to her family by President Jimmy Carter in 1977.

Lois Weber (1881–1939)
First Female Movie Director

Lois Weber started out as a pianist and actress, but ended up a pioneering movie director who oversaw every aspect of her films. Born in Allegheny, Pennsylvania, Weber left home as a teenager to study voice in New York. While appearing in a musical play, she fell in love with the stage manager, Phillips Smalley. They married in 1905 and acted together on stage, but they also became involved in the newest form of entertainment, motion pictures. By 1913, Weber was directing, writing, and acting in an average of one short film per week for Universal Pictures. She later headed her own studio before returning to Universal.

Weber didn't shy away from controversy in her work. Her movies *Where Are My Children?* (1916) and *The Hand That Rocks the Cradle* (1917) promoted birth control, and *The People vs. John Doe* (1916) took issue with police brutality and capital punishment. She examined the dangerous consequences of gossip in *Scandal* (1915), and focused on drug addiction and racial and religious prejudice in other films. In order to tell her stories, Weber made sure she was in complete control. "A real director should be absolute," she told *The Motion Picture Weekly* in 1916. "He alone knows the effects he wants to produce, and he alone should have authority in the arrangement, cutting, titling, or anything else which it may be found necessary to do to the finished product."

For the women above, being first was not an end in itself, but rather a means to realizing an important personal or professional goal. And their accomplishments are just the tip of the iceberg. A complete collection of female firsts would fill a large and heavy book, reminding us that hundreds of dedicated women have made their mark on history—from Mary Kies of South Killingly, Connecticut, the first woman to receive a patent (for a method of weaving straw with silk, in 1809); to Alice Ramsey of Hackensack, New Jersey, the first woman to drive a car across the United States (in 1909); to Ann Bancroft of Scandia, Minnesota, the first woman to ski to both the North Pole (in 1986) and the South Pole (in 1993).

These pioneers inspire us by their example and show us that with the right combination of tenacity and daring, women can do things no one thought possible. "In celebrating women's many achievements we can give girls and women the courage and strength to make a difference," said polar explorer Ann Bancroft. Armed with the fascinating stories of female firsts, we will continue to take chances to follow our dreams.

23

Women Weren't Always in the Books

by Nancy Gruver

Do you ever feel that something's missing when you read a history book and hardly any women are mentioned? Did you know that there used to be even fewer women in history books and English books and civics books? It's true. When I was a girl (more than three decades ago), women didn't merit much mention in any of the traditional subjects that get taught in school. And when women were mentioned, it was usually as mothers or wives of famous men, not as people in their own right. I read every book I could find about women in history and there weren't very many!

Sure, maybe we learned about Clara Barton or Florence Nightingale, but what about Ida B. Wells, Sarah Winnemucca, or Nellie Bly? What about all the women who were active in history? And politics? And medicine? And the arts? And science? What about women who did daring, unusual things? And women who did ordinary, everyday things? Where were they in our studies? Nowhere!

Today we know a lot more about women's achievements and experiences because of the feminist movement. If women had not fought for the vote and many other rights, we might never have gotten to the point where now we can choose to devote our education to learning all about the lives and contributions of women now and in the past. It's called women's studies and only thirty years after the field got started, you can take women's studies classes at almost any college or university. Even high schools and middle schools are starting to offer them.

So what exactly is women's studies? Believe it or not, it's kind of like a sleepover. Having your friends over and talking and talking and talking and talking and . . . Well, you get my point. At a sleepover you can talk about anything and everything. You talk about little things and big things.

The meaning of life and why you despise licorice. Mostly you talk about yourselves—what you think and how you feel and what's happening in your life. Everything is important enough to talk about and nothing is too scary to talk about.

In women's studies, you talk a lot and you listen a lot to everybody else. The topic is YOU and other girls and women. It's all about what it's like to be a girl or a woman (now and in the past). It's about all the things that we do and all the things we care about and how things affect us and change us and how we change them. It's women and girls, A to Z, young and old, all around the world.

Perhaps you wonder why we need to study ourselves. I mean really, don't we already know enough about ourselves? In some ways we do. But in other ways we don't. For instance, we know what it's like to be us, but lots of times we don't know what it's like to be somebody else. We might think we know, but unless that other person has told us themselves (in person or through writing or art), all we're doing is assuming. And there are a lot of things that affect us that we might not really be aware of. Women's studies helps us learn about all these things.

When women's studies started in the late 1960s, it was because of the worldwide movement for women's equal rights. Feminism was opening people's eyes to things that needed to change. Women college students and teachers realized that women's and girls' lives were pretty much invisible in nearly all the classes taught at the time. Even women who were very famous and had great accomplishments were rarely mentioned in textbooks. And "average, everyday women" didn't get any mentions. (Girls' lives were totally invisible, having the double strike of being both kids and female.)

To fill this gap, women college students, especially graduate students, decided to start classes themselves. For instance, in 1969 and 1970 at the State University of New York at Buffalo, a group of women graduate students got together and offered a "bulletin board" class called "Women in Contemporary Society." (A bulletin board class got started by someone posting a notice saying the class was available. If enough students signed up, the class was offered for credit.) Three hundred women signed up, showing a huge interest in this brand-new field of study! Similar things happened on other campuses.

In the beginning, the classes were for women students and taught mainly by women professors, though a few men taught, too. This was done on purpose so women could have their own psychological and physical space to speak and develop their ideas. As women's studies became more accepted and more classes were offered, men began being interested in taking them and public universities decided that they couldn't limit enrollment by gender. In the mid-1980s, women's studies became part of the "general education" classes that students could take to fulfill basic requirements, which also increased the number of men enrolling. At the same time, men were becoming active in the feminist movement and in feminist theory, which led to some men teaching women's studies classes.

On some campuses, like San Diego State University, which set up the first formal women's studies program in 1970, it was professors who started women's studies classes. Sometimes the classes were about women in history (like the only women's studies class my college offered in 1974) or women in literature and were offered in those traditional departments. But students wanted to talk and study about their own lives, too, and what it was like be a woman now and how it affected everything. Soon women's studies began to include classes in health sciences, sociology, psychology, anthropology, economics, philosophy, and many other fields. Today feminist theory is included in virtually every field of academic study.

In the 1970s, it was a very exciting time for the pioneering professors and students. Women greatly enjoyed teaching and taking classes and doing groundbreaking research that focused on women's lives. It was like visiting a country for the first time. There was so much to be learned and discussed. There was also a lot of detective work to be done to find reading and research material for women's studies. (Today there's actually a whole women's studies encyclopedia!) It was the dawn of a new era.

As with most social change, there has been resistance to women's studies. Some colleges and universities said that women's studies wasn't a worthy field of study because women were just people and the classes that taught things from a man's point of view really covered everyone! (That's as ridiculous as saying that Chinese history isn't worth studying because the Chinese are just people, after all, and so American history covers their experience and culture!) But these objections haven't squashed women's studies. In fact, women's studies is the most important reason that women's perspectives and feminist theory are now used in all academic fields. Virtually every part of colleges and universities has been changed by the fact that women demanded to be included everywhere.

In 1972, a handful of colleges and universities offered women's studies as a major, which was a huge step forward in increasing the acceptance of the field as legitimate. In 2001, there were more than 735 colleges and universities that had women's studies programs. About forty of those programs offered graduate degrees and about ten offered Ph.D.'s. Women's studies has also taken root all around the world, just like the women's movement.

What's next for women's studies? People who teach it are focused on making the field truly diverse, racially, culturally, and socio-economically, both in what it studies and who studies and teaches it. My own hope is that in the decades to come, women's studies will include more and more girls' studies and become a class you can take in middle school and high school, wherever you are. There's still a lot to learn!

Time Matters by E. Susan Barber

Students ask me all the time if dates are important. I tell them that a time line can be a useful way of understanding the history of a particular movement or event. This time line focuses on women's political, social, and economic history in the U.S. in the eighteenth, nineteenth, and twentieth centuries. It begins with the first political organizations by Anglo-American women during the American Revolution and concludes with the Second Feminist Expo, an international conference of women activists concerned with contemporary issues affecting women across the globe. This time line shows that women's history does not always reflect continuous forward progress. There are also defeats or reverses. And sometimes the gains of one particular group of women come at the expense of women of another race or class.

The 18th Century

1774

• The Edenton Ladies' Petition. Fifty-one women in Edenton, North Carolina, support the American patriots by refusing to purchase or use goods imported from England.

• Abigail Adams writes a letter to her husband, John, in Philadelphia, asking that he and the other men who were at work on the Declaration of Independence "Remember the Ladies." John replies with humor. In its final form, the Declaration states that "all men are created equal."

1790

• Judith Sargent Stevens Murray publishes "On the Equality of the Sexes," which advocates that women and men should have equal educations.

1792

• *Vindication of the Rights of Woman* by Mary Wollstonecraft (whose daughter, Mary Shelley, wrote *Frankenstein*) is published in the U.S. With its advocacy for equal opportunity for women in education and other realms of life, this book becomes an inspiration and key text for 19th-century feminists.

1793

• Catharine Littlefield Greene helps Eli Whitney perfect the cotton gin, but her name is left off the patent application. The cotton gin, which sped up the process of cleaning cotton, contributed to the increase in the population of enslaved women (and men) and put more slave women to work cultivating cotton. It also stimulated the development of the New England textile mills.

24

- A group of free black women form the Female Anti-Slavery Society of Salem, Massachusetts. During the 1830s, several other female anti-slavery organizations are started—some all-black, some all-white, some interracial.

- The first women's rights convention in the United States is held in Seneca Falls, New York.

1848

1832

- Mary Lyon founds Mount Holyoke College in Massachusetts, the first four-year college for women in the U.S.

1837

The 19th Century

1839

1821

- A group of investors establishes the first textile mill in Lowell, Massachusetts. Over the next 40 years, the Lowell mills will employ thousands of girls and women from the surrounding countryside.
- Emma Hart Willard founds the Troy Female Seminary in New York—the first endowed school for girls.

- Mississippi passes the first Married Woman's Property Act, which permitted married women to own property in their own names.

1844

- Female textile workers in Massachusetts organize the Lowell Female Labor Reform Association (LFLRA), one of the first permanent labor associations for working women in the U.S.

1833

- Oberlin College in Ohio becomes the first coeducational college in the United States. In 1841, Oberlin awards the first academic degrees to women. Early graduates include future suffragists Lucy Stone and Antoinette Brown.

- Amelia Jenks Bloomer launches the very controversial dress reform movement with a costume bearing her name. Most Bloomer costumes had full "Turkish trousers" and a knee-length overdress.
- Female Medical College is founded in Philadelphia, Pennsylvania, by a group of Quakers. When the college became coed in the late 1960s, its name was changed to the Medical College of Pennsylvania.

- The women's rights movement splits into two factions because of disagreements over the 14th and soon-to-be-ratified 15th Amendment (1870), which granted black men the right to vote. Elizabeth Cady Stanton and Susan B. Anthony form the more radical New York–based National Woman Suffrage Association (NWSA). Lucy Stone, Henry Blackwell, and Julia Ward Howe organize the more conservative American Woman Suffrage Association (AWSA), which is centered in Boston.
- Wyoming becomes the first territory that is organized with a woman suffrage provision. In 1890, Wyoming will be admitted to the Union with its suffrage provision intact.

1850

1869

1851

- Former slave Sojourner Truth speaks about slavery and woman suffrage before a spellbound audience at a women's rights convention in Akron, Ohio.

1865

- The 13th Amendment ends slavery. Newly emancipated Southern black women form thousands of organizations aimed at "uplifting the race."

1868

- The 14th Amendment is ratified, which extends to all citizens the protections of the Constitution against unjust state laws. This amendment was the first to define "citizens" and "voters" as male.

1861–1865

- The American Civil War disrupts suffrage activity as women, North and South, divert their energies to war work. The war itself, however, serves as a training ground, as women gain important organizational and occupational skills they will use after the war.

1866

- Elizabeth Cady Stanton and Susan B. Anthony form the American Equal Rights Association, an organization for white and black women and men dedicated to the goal of universal suffrage.

• NWSA refuses to work for the ratification of the 15th Amendment because it excludes women. Frederick Douglass severs his association with Elizabeth Cady Stanton and Susan B. Anthony over NWSA's position.

1870

• Attorney Myra Bradwell sues in the U.S. Supreme Court for the right to practice law in Illinois. Her case is rejected because she is a married woman.
• The typewriter is invented. During the last quarter of the 19th century, more and more women will be employed as clerical workers.

• A Woman Suffrage Amendment is introduced in the United States Congress. The wording is unchanged in 1919 when the amendment finally passes both houses and becomes the 19th Amendment.

1873

1878

1876

• The telephone is invented. In 1878, the Boston Telephone Despatch Company begins hiring female operators because they are more easily controlled and will work for less money than male operators.

1874

• Annie Wittenmyer founds the Woman's Christian Temperance Union (WCTU). With Frances Willard at its head (beginning in 1879), the WCTU will become an important force in the fight for woman suffrage.

1872

• Victoria Woodhull is the first woman to campaign for the U.S. presidency.
• Susan B. Anthony is arrested and brought to trial in Rochester, New York, for attempting to vote for Ulysses S. Grant in the presidential election. At the same time, Sojourner Truth is turned away from a polling booth in Grand Rapids, Michigan.

1883

- *Ladies' Home Journal* begins publication.

1895

- Elizabeth Cady Stanton publishes The *Woman's Bible,* which criticizes the role defined for women in the organized churches.

1889

- Jane Addams and Ellen Gates Starr found Hull House, a settlement house project in Chicago's 19th Ward. Their action inspires women around the country to start similar projects. The growth of these settlement houses shifted the American political agenda to focus more on women's and children's issues, which, in turn, created the political climate in which the 19th Amendment could be ratified.

1896

- Mary Church Terrell, Ida B. Wells-Barnett, Margaret Murray Washington, Fanny Jackson Coppin, Frances Ellen Watkins Harper, Charlotte Forten Grimké, and Harriet Tubman meet in Washington, D.C., to form the National Association of Colored Women (NACW).

1890

- NWSA and AWSA are reunited as the National American Woman Suffrage Association (NAWSA) under the leadership of Elizabeth Cady Stanton.

1893

- Hannah Greenbaum Solomon founds the National Council of Jewish Women (NCJW).
- Kansas lawyer and agrarian activist Mary Elizabeth Lease runs unsuccessfully for the U.S. Senate on the Populist Party ticket.

1903

- Mary Dreier, Rheta Childe Dorr, Leonora O'Reilly, and others form the Women's Trade Union League (WTUL) of New York, an organization of middle-class and working-class women. This group will become a nucleus of the International Ladies' Garment Workers' Union (ILGWU).

1892

- Ida B. Wells launches her nationwide anti-lynching campaign after the murder of three black businessmen in Memphis, Tennessee.

• The U.S. Supreme Court decides *Muller* v. *Oregon*. In its decision the Court claimed that because women were mothers or potential mothers, the number of hours they work should be limited to ten per day. This decision caused hardships for many laboring women, who now had to do additional work at home—taking in laundry, preparing and selling food, doing sewing—to contribute to their family's income.

1908

• The National Federation of Women's Clubs—which by this time includes more than two million white women and women of color throughout the United States—formally endorses the suffrage campaign.

1914

The 20th Century

• The Woman's Peace Party is founded.

1915

1909

• "Uprising of the 20,000." Shirtwaist makers in New York City strike for better wages and working conditions. They are supported by the WTUL, but they are unsuccessful.

1913

• Alice Paul and Lucy Burns organize the Congressional Union, later known as the National Woman's Party (1916). Using radical militant tactics, members of the Woman's Party participate in hunger strikes, picket the White House, and engage in other forms of civil disobedience to publicize the suffrage cause.

1911

• The National Association Opposed to Woman Suffrage (NAOWS) is organized. Led by Mrs. Arthur Dodge, its members include wealthy, influential women and some Catholic clergymen—including Cardinal Gibbons, who, in 1916, sent an address to NAOWS's convention in Washington, D.C. In addition to the distillers and brewers, who worked largely behind the scenes, the "antis" also draw support from urban political machines, Southern congressmen, and corporate capitalists—like railroad magnates and meatpackers—who support the "antis" by contributing to their war chests.

- NAWSA president Carrie Chapman Catt unveils her "winning plan" for suffrage at a convention in Atlantic City, New Jersey. Catt's strategy is a well-organized campaign that combines the efforts of thousands of suffragists involved in local and state suffrage campaign initiatives with a national campaign to ratify the 19th Amendment.
- Jeannette Rankin of Montana becomes the first woman to represent her state in the U.S. House of Representatives.

1916

- The 19th Amendment is ratified on August 18 and added to the Constitution on August 26. Now that women have the right to vote nationally, NAWSA ceases to exist, but its organization becomes the nucleus of the League of Women Voters.

1920

- Babe Didrikson wins three Olympic medals in the women's high jump, the 80-meter hurdle, and the javelin throw. Four years earlier, 16-year-old Betty Robinson became the first U.S. woman to win a medal at the Olympic Games, for the 100-meter dash.
- Amelia Earhart is the first woman to fly solo across the Atlantic.
- Frances Perkins becomes Secretary of Labor in Franklin D. Roosevelt's administration, the first woman to hold a Cabinet position.

1932

1921

- Margaret Sanger founds the American Birth Control League.
- The Sheppard-Towner Act provides public health nurses to bring prenatal and infant care to women in impoverished communities across the nation.

1939

- African American soloist Marian Anderson sings on the steps of the Lincoln Memorial after being denied permission to perform at the Daughters of the American Revolution's (DAR) Constitution Hall. A major force behind the Lincoln Memorial concert was Eleanor Roosevelt, who resigned her DAR membership in protest of its treatment of Anderson.

1923

- The National Woman's Party first proposes the Equal Rights Amendment (ERA) to eliminate discrimination on the basis of gender. It has still never been ratified.

• Thousands of black and white "Rosie the Riveters" manufacture bombers and battleships during World War II.

1941–1945

• The baby boom begins after thousands of "Rosie the Riveters" are asked to leave their more profitable wartime jobs and thousands of G.I.s return home from the war, move to the suburbs (in many cases thanks to the G.I. Bill), and begin raising families.

1945–1950

• Nearly 350,000 women serve during World War II in women's branches of the Army (WACs), the Navy (WAVES), and the Air Force (WASPs).

1942–1943

• Simone de Beauvoir's *The Second Sex,* a wide-ranging, philosophical discussion of feminism and women's subordinate role in society, is published in the United States.

1953

1943

• The Equal Pay Act is first introduced in Congress.

1942

• Jeanne Wakatsuki and thousands of Japanese American women and girls living on the West Coast of the U.S. are sent, with their families, to internment camps amid fears they might be disloyal to the U.S. during World War II. As Jeanne Wakatsuki Houston, she later wrote about her experiences in *Farewell to Manzanar.*

1955

• Rosa Parks refuses to give up her seat to a white person on a bus in Montgomery, Alabama, and is arrested. Her defiance seeds the famous Montgomery bus boycott.
• WHER—1430 on the AM dial—debuts. This first all-girl radio station (based in Memphis, Tennessee) will go off the air in 1966.
• Del Martin and Phyllis Lyon found the Daughters of Bilitis, the first lesbian rights group in the United States.

1947

• Psychiatrist Marynia Farnham and sociologist Ferdinand Lundberg publish *Modern Woman: The Lost Sex,* which emphasized the importance of women's roles as mothers and labeled women who competed with men "neurotic."

- Dolores Huerta helps found the United Farm Workers.
- Rachel Carson's book *Silent Spring* is published, sparking the environmental movement.
- Mississippi sharecropper Fannie Lou Hamer leads a group of her neighbors to register to vote and is jailed and severely beaten by the police. Despite death threats, Hamer continues her activism, becoming a field secretary for SNCC and co-founding the Mississippi Freedom Democratic Party (MFDP). Her courage inspires others to join the civil rights crusade and gives rise to more grassroots leaders.

1962

- The Civil Rights Act is passed. Title VII of the act contains a clause that forbids discrimination on the basis of sex.

1964

- The first women's studies course is offered, at Cornell University in New York.

- Gloria Steinem and Pat Carbine launch *Ms.* magazine.

1969

1971

1963

- President Kennedy's Commission on the Status of Women, led by Eleanor Roosevelt and Esther Peterson, reveals continued widespread inequality and discrimination for women in employment and the law.
- The Equal Pay Act is finally passed by Congress. It prohibits discrimination in pay on the basis of sex.
- Betty Friedan publishes *The Feminine Mystique,* a catalyst of the "second wave" of feminism.

1972

- The ERA is passed by both houses of Congress. Within a year, 22 states—of the needed 38—have ratified it.
- Phyllis Schlafly, a conservative political activist who ran, unsuccessfully, for Congress, organizes Stop ERA.
- Congress passes the Education Amendments. Title IX of that bill prohibits gender-based discrimination in educational activities that receive federal funds.
- "I Am Woman" by Helen Reddy becomes the anthem of the feminist movement.

1960

- The Food and Drug Administration approves the birth control pill, the first contraception that enables women to have reliable control of their reproduction.

- *Roe* v. *Wade* is decided by the U.S. Supreme Court, legalizing abortion during the first trimester of pregnancy.
- The "Battle of the Sexes." On September 20, at the Houston Astrodome, Billie Jean King beats Bobby Riggs in a highly publicized match that was telecast nationally. King's triumph empowered female athletes, tennis players in particular.

1973

- International Woman of the Year (IWY) Conference in Houston, Texas—chaired by Bella Abzug and attended by First Ladies Lady Bird Johnson, Betty Ford, and Rosalynn Carter—reveals deep ideological divisions between pro-ERA groups and anti-ERA groups.

1977

- Ronald Reagan is elected President of the United States by significantly more male voters than female voters. This difference in voting preference marks the emergence of a women's voting bloc—called the "gender gap"—for the first time since the 19th Amendment was ratified. From this point on, this gender gap will be evident in the ways in which women voters consistently vote in support of issues that concern them as women.
- National Women's History Project is founded.

1980

1981

- 21-year-old Chinese-American architectural design student Maya Lin wins the competition for the design of the Vietnam Veterans Memorial in Washington, D.C.

1982

- The ERA goes down to defeat, three states short of its goal.

1974

- Artist Judy Chicago begins work on "The Dinner Party," a representation of women's history from the prehistoric age to the 20th century. "The Dinner Party," which involved the work of more than a hundred skilled craftspeople, was completed in 1979 and first exhibited at the San Francisco Museum of Modern Art in 1979.
- Six hundred Catholic nuns meeting at the National Leadership Conference of Women Religious adopt a resolution asking their church to ordain women as priests.

1984

- Geraldine Ferraro (Democrat-NY) becomes the first woman to run as a vice-presidential candidate on a national party ticket.

159

- Take Our Daughters to Work® Day is launched.

1993

- Congress passes the Violence Against Women Act, which provides funding for state programs to create rape crisis centers, sexual assault hotlines, and women's shelters.

1994

- Anita Hill testifies before the Senate Judiciary Committee, charging Supreme Court nominee Clarence Thomas with sexual harassment. Despite her testimony, Thomas is confirmed, but the incident brings the issue of sexual harassment to the forefront.

- First Feminist Expo held in Washington, D.C.

1996

- Second Feminist Expo held in Baltimore, Maryland.

1991

2000

1987

- Wilma Mankiller is the first woman to be elected Principal Chief of the Cherokee Nation of Oklahoma.
- Through a congressional resolution, March is declared "Women's History Month."

1997

- Sarah McLachlan launches the first Lilith Fair, a transcontinental women's music festival.

1998

1985

- Ellen Malcolm founds EMILY's List (Early Money Is Like Yeast) to provide campaign funds for Democratic, female, pro-choice candidates.

- Congress passes the Violence Against Women Act II, which extends additional funding to sexual assault programs, with an emphasis on the violence against women in the workforce, on college campuses, and in the military.
- *Time* magazine cover story: "Is Feminism Dead?"

by Paula A. Treckel

The Facets of Feminism

fem·i·nisms (fem´uh niz´umz), n., plural.

1. doctrines advocating social and political rights for women equal to those of men.

2. organized movements for the attainment of such rights for women.

> **Liberal feminist:** one who utilizes the government and institutions to bring about the equality of women and men.
>
> **Radical feminist:** one who advocates the transformation or overthrow of institutions that oppress women.
>
> **Cultural feminist:** one who celebrates the differences between women and men and supports the creation of a female "counterculture."
>
> **Womanist:** one who bridges the boundaries between women of color and celebrates their diversity.
>
> **Marxist feminist:** one who sees class struggle as the root of women's oppression and works toward class revolution.
>
> **Global feminist:** one who sees the women of the world as one and works to end their oppression everywhere.
>
> **Ecofeminist:** one who believes women have a special relationship to nature and a responsibility to act as caretakers of the environment.

Feminists come in all shapes and sizes, all races, creeds, and colors.

There are young feminists and old feminists, male feminists and female feminists, rich feminists and poor feminists.

There are feminists who are Democrats, feminists who are Republicans, and some who are Independents, too.

There are feminists who believe in the "Right to Life," and there are feminists who believe in women's right to choose.

Some feminists like wearing makeup and fashionable "feminine" clothing; others dress for comfort rather than for style.

Some feminists love and have women partners and some feminists love and have men partners.

Some married feminists proudly take their husbands' names while others proudly keep their own.

Some feminists' life goal is to marry and raise families while other feminists want to devote themselves solely to careers.

In other words, there are as many different kinds of feminists as there are feminisms. We aren't all alike.

While there is no special test you have to take to qualify as a feminist, people who call themselves feminists share a few basic beliefs. They believe in the fundamental equality of women and men. They believe that all girls should grow up in a world that allows them to explore, fully, their abilities and interests, follow their dreams, wherever they might lead them.

The fact is, feminism is a big tent large enough to hold a wide variety of people.

So, why aren't more young women proud or even willing to call themselves "feminists"? Perhaps because they believe that there is no longer any need for them to be one. Or because they think that there is only one kind.

But that isn't so.

Some girls don't really understand the meaning of the word *feminist*. They think it is a bad word. A word that identifies them as a person who is ugly and angry and hates boys. They think that to be a feminist means to discriminate against men.

And who wants to be seen as ugly and angry and mean?

More than 150 years ago, in 1848, a group of women and men, including Elizabeth Cady Stanton, Lucretia Mott, and former slave Frederick Douglass, met in Seneca Falls, New York, and organized the first women's rights convention in America. At this convention the American feminist movement was born. This later became known as the "first wave" of feminism.

From the very beginning of the women's rights movement, feminists were called "man haters." Women who supported the movement were denounced as "selfish," "unladylike," and mocked as "ugly old maids." They were even labeled "un-American" for asserting their rights as citizens. Those who felt threatened by the women's rights movement hoped to scare their supporters away by calling feminists bad names. But despite their efforts, more and more people joined the women's rights campaign.

By the beginning of the twentieth century, lots of people—men as well as women—had joined in support of women's right to vote. But once women got that right, many believed their work was done. Many left the movement, thinking women now had all the rights they required.

This was not the case. And as new generations of girls came of age, they discovered that simply having the right to vote was not enough.

During the Roaring Twenties, the Great Depression, and the two world wars, some American women fought to keep the rights they had gained as they worked to help support their families and their country. But after the Second

World War, many women grew tired of the fight. They retreated to their suburban homes and raised a new generation of American girls and boys. At the same time, these middle-class housewives and moms began to grow dissatisfied with their lives. They wanted more.

Then, in 1963, Betty Friedan dropped a bombshell. She came out with a book, *The Feminine Mystique,* that identified women's dissatisfaction with their lives and sparked the rebirth of feminism in America. This began the "second wave" of feminism.

Just as in the nineteenth century, the new feminist movement was inspired by the civil rights movement of the day. Many people working for the civil rights of African Americans during the 1950s and 1960s came to understand the limits on women's rights in the United States. And so they worked to end discrimination on the basis of both race and sex.

In 1966, Betty Friedan and other feminists founded the National Organization for Women (NOW). This organization still stands at the forefront of the American feminist movement. It is the leader in securing and defending women's legal rights in the United States, regardless of their race, creed, color, or sexual preference. It represents "liberal feminists"—those who work within our existing government to improve women's lives by changing laws or establishing new ones.

At the same time, the children of post–WWII America, the baby boom generation, began to question the values of their parents. The continued oppression of African Americans and controversy over the war in Vietnam led many young people to challenge authority. As more and more young women became involved in these protest movements on college campuses across the land, they also became aware of the sexism of their male peers. They held consciousness-raising sessions to educate themselves and others about the sexism around them. They founded the women's liberation movement.

These young radical women believed that "the personal is political"—that women's personal actions and beliefs have a much larger, political impact—and they fought to make themselves accepted, understood, and respected. They believed that America's governmental system would not accommodate their demands, and so they advocated its change. They worked for "women's liberation," not just their equality. Some even advocated revolution.

Many young "radical" feminists loudly demonstrated against the institutions—religious groups, colleges and universities, the media, the government—that they believed oppressed American women. For example, in 1968 they picketed the Miss America Pageant, protesting what they considered the sexual exploitation of women. In 1970, they staged a sit-in at the offices of the *Ladies' Home Journal,* demanding that its editors publish a special issue addressing women's legal rights and status. (The magazine complied, and this special issue of the *Ladies' Home Journal* was very popular and inspired the founding of *Ms.* magazine by Gloria Steinem and others.) Radical feminists also staged marches in Washington, D.C., confronted their opponents, and refused to back down. On college campuses they demanded courses be taught about women's history—"her-story," they called it. How could they plan their futures, they asked, if they didn't know their past? In their dress and in their manners, they intentionally violated the "ladylike" behavior their mothers' had taught them. And they advocated an end to the double standard between men's and women's social behavior.

IT BEGINS WHILE YOU SINK IN HIS ARMS AND ENDS WITH YOUR ARMS IN HIS SINK

Radical feminist writers like Kate Millett, Shulamith Firestone, and Robin Morgan wrote important theoretical works identifying the "dialectic of sex" and exploring the "sexual politics" of the day. Their goal was to forge a new "sisterhood" of women in America. They even inspired some radical feminists to create a counterculture of their own. A world of women separate from that of men.

"Cultural feminists" celebrate women's differences from men. They have created an environment in which women can express themselves artistically, make new kinds of music, and laugh at their own forms of humor. From sculptor Judy Chicago's multimedia installation "The Dinner Party" to the musical festival Lilith Fair to Eve Ensler's theater piece *The Vagina Monologues*, "cultural feminism" has enriched our world. Many women of color have felt excluded by what they see as a white middle-class feminist movement. In her book *In Search of Our Mothers' Gardens*, writer Alice Walker created the word *womanist* to link women of color with black feminists and celebrate the diversity of women's experiences. The goal of womanists is inclusion. They work to build bridges between women so that the problems of race, sex, class, and power may be overcome.

Some women believe that capitalism—the way our economy works—is at the heart of women's oppression. They call themselves "Marxist feminists" and believe that class revolution will resolve the sexism in our world.

Others feminists recognize that "sisterhood" is not limited by national boundaries. It must and should unite women around the world. American women have much to learn from women in other countries, including those less developed than our own.

"Global feminism" began with the first World Conference on Women held in Mexico in 1975. It works to solve "the world's problems as if women mattered." Global feminists, for example, campaigned to redefine rape as a war crime when it takes place during a time of military conflict and convinced Western nations to grant political asylum to women fleeing the violence of their husbands or family members. A concern for human rights, they argue, must include concern for women's rights, too.

"Ecofeminists" believe men's destruction of nature reflects men's domination of women. They urge us to rethink our relationship to our planet. Women, they believe, have a deep spiritual connection to nature and a responsibility to sustain our Mother Earth. In caring for our world, we care for ourselves.

Since the rebirth of the women's movement in the 1960s, many American feminists have worked for passage of the Equal Rights Amendment (ERA), first proposed before Congress in 1923 by Alice Paul. Some have worked to liberalize laws regarding women's right to abortion, a right legalized in 1973 with the U.S. Supreme Court decision *Roe* v. *Wade*. Others have championed the rights of lesbians. These have been controversial campaigns. Not all agree that women should have the right to abortions. And many women remain uncomfortable supporting lesbians' rights. Their disagreement is proof again that not all feminists think alike. But this basic freedom—of women to have opinions and to disagree—was also a right fought for by feminists in our collective past.

During the 1980s many Americans were disturbed by the gains made by American women. They wanted to turn back the clock on women's rights. But Susan Faludi's book *Backlash* educated women about this campaign against the feminist movement. And Naomi Wolf's *The Beauty Myth* introduced a new generation of American women to the many problems and issues facing them today. As a result, these young women have injected new energy and enthusiasm into the feminist movement. Has a "third wave" of American feminism begun?

American girls of the twenty-first century have opportunities to study, to play, to live, and to dream. Opportunities that are the result of the efforts of women and men who have lived before them. Because of these people who proudly called themselves "feminists," today's girls have the right to make choices about their "tomorrows."

So . . . what kind of a feminist will you be?

26

MEN CAN BE *Feminists*, TOO

by NOMAS

From the founding of this nation until today, there have been American men who have championed the women's rights movement and cheered women's progress and the victories against oppression and second-class status. Among these were **Frederick Douglass**, *who, with his wife, Anna Murray Douglass, worked for equal rights for all people, and* **James Mott**, *husband of Lucretia Coffin Mott and co-creator in 1848 of the first women's rights convention in the United States. In the early twentieth century, there were four-term governor of New York* **Al Smith** *and Susan B. Anthony's nephew, Kansas representative* **Daniel Anthony**, *who introduced the Equal Rights Amendment to Congress in 1923. Later in the century, actors* **Alan Alda** *and* **Ed Asner** *and scholar* **Cornel West** *were among the men who stood alongside and behind women on the march for equal opportunity.*

There have also been men's organizations that have proudly proclaimed themselves pro-feminist. Among them are Men Against Domestic Violence, Men Against Pornography, and the Colorado-based collective NOMAS (National Organization for Men Against Sexism), which adheres to the following pro-feminist tenet:

Whatever psychological burdens men have to overcome, women are still the most universal and direct victims of our patriarchy. Our organization takes a highly visible and energetic position in support of women's struggle for equality.

—Photo The Pictorial News Co.

EIGHTY-FIVE COURAGEOUS AND CONVINCED MEN

s picture shows the "men's division" of the suffrage parade in New York. They found the chaffing of the crowd that lined the streets "inspiring."

Our movement was born directly out of, and is continually nourished by, feminism. Even if we could not see any pragmatic ways in which we, as men, could benefit from an end to traditional patriarchy (and we can see many), most of us would strongly support women's struggle, simply because it is so unquestionably just and right. Our support for women's rights and specific women's issues is therefore vigorous and unmistakable.

The simple truth is that the oppression of women, homophobia and the oppression of homosexuals, subtle or blatant racism, and numerous wounds and sex role burdens placed on men in our society are all part of the institution of patriarchy. Each injustice associated with sex, gender or race contributes to all of the others. All oppressions are linked, and an active consciousness of any oppression leads to an awareness of them all.

The uniqueness and great potential strength of our movement is that we focus on all these categories of oppressions. Most people in this country have never heard gay men speak up for women's rights. Few people have heard heterosexual men speak out forcefully for the civil rights of gay men and lesbians. Most people have not heard women speak knowledgeably and sympathetically about men's sex role burdens. With NOMAS, these sorts of expressions take place at every conference or meeting. There is something very special and wonderful in the breadth of our vision as a social movement which speaks more persuasively than any of us could do alone. The totality of our opposition to the consequences of patriarchy is our greatest strength.

We are not standing up as men to create a movement that cares only about men's sex role issues, or only about gay rights, or only about supporting women's fight against sexism. What is special about our movement is that we can see the connections between all these injustices, and are committed to ending them all.

We strongly support the continuing struggle of women for full equality, in the U.S. and around the world. We stand as allies of feminist women in opposing male supremacy, and in working against economic and legal discrimination, domestic abuse, harassment, rape, and other long-standing injustices. We welcome women as members of NOMAS. We ask men to see, name, and to challenge male privilege in our daily lives.

27

The positive changes in the status of American women over the last 150 years has not been the work of a few, but of hundreds—thousands—of indefatigable souls. Some promoted suffrage before suffrage was cool; others insisted on equality in the workplace; still more challenged the status quo on behalf of women of color. Here are snapshots of some you may have not yet encountered.

The Roll Call of Crusaders

by Fran Ellers

Nineteenth Century

The Grimké Sisters, Sarah (1792–1873) and **Angelina** (1805–79), came to despise slavery even though they were the privileged daughters of a South Carolina slaveholder. They later moved north and became the first women to speak publicly against slavery to mixed audiences (men and women seated together—not the norm at the time). They also campaigned for equal rights for women, arguing that women deserved the same education and voting rights as men. Their activism helped pave the way for Elizabeth Cady Stanton, Susan B. Anthony, and Lucretia Mott.

Esther Hobart Morris (1814–1902), who had moved to the Wyoming Territory with her husband during the gold rush of the mid-1800s, thought legalizing the vote for women would be a great way for Wyoming to advertise itself. Her lobbying helped influence Wyoming lawmakers, and in 1869 Wyoming became the first state to grant women the right to vote in all elections. The next year, Morris became the first woman in the history of the United States to be appointed as justice of the peace.

The Blackwell family included three of the most accomplished women of the nineteenth century. *Elizabeth* (1821–1910), the first woman to earn an M.D., and her sister *Emily* (1826–1910), also a physician, opened the first American hospital for women and staffed completely by women; they also founded a women's medical college. *Antoinette Brown Blackwell* (1825–1921), their sister-in-law, became the first American woman to be ordained as a minister. Antoinette, also an outspoken opponent of slavery and proponent of suffrage, later wrote books making scientific arguments for the equality of the sexes.

Jane Cunningham Croly (1829–1901) was a syndicated columnist and newspaper editor in 1868 when she and other women journalists were barred from hearing Charles Dickens speak at the New York Press Club. So Croly started her own club for her own gender. Twenty years later, she organized women's clubs across the nation into the General Federation of Women's Clubs, which is still active today.

Frances Ellen Watkins Harper (1825–1911) was the leading black writer of her time and is credited with introducing the tradition of African American protest poems to a larger audience; she also wrote novels and essays. Active in the Underground Railroad and other anti-slavery efforts as a young woman, she later toured the South speaking on behalf of suffrage, women's education, and the welfare of newly freed black women.

Belva Ann Lockwood (1830–1917) spent five years lobbying Congress to pass a law to allow women attorneys to practice before the U.S. Supreme Court. The law finally passed, and Lockwood became the first woman to argue a Supreme Court case; she also sponsored the first Southern black person to practice before the court. Lockwood also successfully lobbied for a law to require equal pay for equal work by civil service employees—and ran twice, unsuccessfully, for president (in 1884 and 1888).

Louisa May Alcott (1832–88) took adolescent girls seriously enough to write novels about them, including the classic *Little Women*. Alcott was also serious about women's rights: She used her clout as a popular author to promote women's suffrage and was first to register at the polls in her hometown of Concord, Massachusetts, after Massachusetts women won the right to vote on taxes and other community issues.

Kate Mullaney (1845–1906) got a job in a Troy, New York, laundry when she was nineteen. For working at least twelve hours a day, six days a week, she earned about $3—less if she damaged a collar. To protest the low wages and dangerous working conditions, she organized the first female labor union in the country and led two hundred of her fellow laundresses in a strike. They got a 25-percent raise, and Mullaney went on to become a national labor leader, pushing for workers' and women's rights.

Frances Willard (1839–98) climbed the academic ladder all the way to the top and was a president by the time she was thirty-six of Evanston (Illinois) College for Ladies, which later merged with Northwestern University. But in 1874, she gave all that up to become a leader in the Woman's Christian Temperance Union. The WCTU worked to ban the sale of alcohol in America, and under Willard it became the largest organization of women in the country. At the same time Willard broadened its vision. She encouraged members to support suffrage so they could vote for their causes. The WCTU also supported many social reforms, including equal pay for equal work, the eight-hour day, and world peace.

Josephine St. Pierre Ruffin (1842–1924) got married when she was sixteen and moved with her husband, George, to England—as African Americans, they refused to raise their children in a country that embraced slavery. But as the abolitionist movement gained ground, they moved back to be a part of it. Josephine helped recruit soldiers for the Union Army and later got involved in women's suffrage efforts. She was particularly interested in the lives of black women, organizing clubs and groups that eventually became the National Association of Colored Women.

Early Twentieth Century

Anna Julia Cooper (1858–1964) established herself as a leading intellectual when she published "A Voice from the South by a Black Woman from the South" in 1892, which was in part a call for higher education for black women. She pursued that aim for the rest of her life: as principal of the nation's premier black high school, in Washington, D.C. (the M Street School); as an organizer of the Colored Women's YWCA; as founder of Frelinghuysen University in Washington for working-class African Americans; and as the recipient of a doctorate—in her mid-sixties—from the Sorbonne in Paris. Along the way Cooper, who was widowed, raised her half brother's five orphaned grandchildren.

Mary Church Terrell (1863–1954) was an advocate for gender and racial equality throughout her life. A leader of the National Association of Colored Women, she joined white women's groups in the famous suffrage parade on the day of Woodrow Wilson's inauguration in 1913—even though she was relegated to the back of the march—and in picketing the White House in 1917. She's also well known for what she did as an old woman—she forced the integration of lunch counters and restaurants in Washington, D.C. On February 28, 1950, the eighty-seven-year-old Terrell and her colleagues entered the segregated Thompson Restaurant; as expected, they were refused service. The lawsuit they filed in protest led to a court's declaring segregated eating places in the nation's capital unconstitutional.

Mary McLeod Bethune (1875–1955) had all of $1.50 to spend when she started a school for African American girls in Daytona Beach, Florida, in 1904. But this dynamic speaker ultimately raised enough money to turn her school into a college and made herself heard all the way to Washington, D.C., where she advised President Franklin D. Roosevelt on minority affairs. An avid organizer, she also founded the National Council of Negro Women.

Maud Younger (1870–1936) inherited a fortune from her wealthy California family, but her life took an unexpected turn when she was twenty-one. That was the year she visited the New York City College Settlement, which helped educate and socialize immigrants. She planned to stay about a week, but lived there for five years, then went to work as a waitress as part of her effort to learn more about the lives of working people. She eventually organized a waitresses' union in San Francisco and helped push through California's eight-hour-day law before turning her efforts to the national fight for women's suffrage and equal rights.

Crystal Eastman (1881–1928), one of the few female lawyers at the turn of the twentieth century, believed passionately in protecting the civil rights of people without political or financial power. She wrote the country's first law to compensate workers for on-the-job injuries (which passed) and was one of four authors of the country's first Equal Rights Amendment (which didn't). She also helped start the country's best-known advocacy group for the legally disenfranchised, the American Civil Liberties Union.

Inez Milholland Boissevain (1886–1916) became a martyr of the suffrage movement when she died after collapsing during a speech in 1916. Boissevain, then thirty and a lawyer, was on a tour of the western United States to urge the defeat of President Woodrow Wilson for reelection because he hadn't endorsed suffrage. She was already a symbol of the movement as the striking woman who led a suffrage parade on a white horse on the day of Wilson's inauguration in 1913. By then, she'd been an activist for years: As a college student at Vassar, Boissevain held a suffrage rally at a nearby cemetery after the school refused to allow it on campus.

Esther Peterson (1906–97) witnessed the Utah railroad strike when she was twelve years old, an experience that changed her life. She became a labor activist who was particularly interested in improving working conditions for women. Ultimately, as an assistant secretary of labor in the early 1960s, she led the successful campaign for a federal law guaranteeing that women and men get equal pay for equal work.

Later Twentieth Century

Mary Hallaren (1907–) enlisted in the Army in 1942, and when the recruiter asked her what someone as short as she (4'10") could do, she reportedly replied, "You don't have to be six feet tall to have a brain that works." Hallaren eventually led the first Women's Army Corps (WAC) battalion during World War II and became the WAC director after the war. In 1948, she helped women win the right to serve in the military in peacetime.

Florynce "Flo" Kennedy (1916–2000) threatened a lawsuit when Columbia Law School refused to admit her and went on to become that school's first black female graduate. Law degree in hand, she helped force the New York legislature to liberalize the state's abortion law, founded the Feminist Party, helped start the National Women's Political Caucus, and led a mass urination to protest the lack of women's rest rooms at Harvard University.

Dolores Huerta (1930–), a role model for Mexican American women, was a single mother of seven children in 1962 when she helped Cesar Chavez form what became the United Farm Workers. Working at first on behalf of Mexican and other families who took seasonal jobs with the grape growers, Huerta organized strikes and boycotts, negotiated contracts, and lobbied for political change for farm workers throughout California and the U.S. As a result, children of migrant workers began receiving government services and the workers themselves won unemployment insurance, collective bargaining, and immigration rights. Huerta enlisted feminists, students, and other groups in her efforts to help migrant workers, and later returned the favor by taking leadership roles in organizations dedicated to equality for women.

Ruth Bader Ginsburg (1933–) created the Women's Rights Project of the American Civil Liberties Union in the early 1970s in hopes of winning court victories in sex discrimination cases. By the end of the decade she had argued six such cases before the U.S. Supreme Court and won five of them. Today she sits on the Supreme Court herself, only the second woman in history to do so.

Byllye Avery (1937–), a leading women's health advocate since the 1970s, was the widowed mother of two small children in 1976 when she and three other women each took out a $2,000 credit-union loan and a line of credit at Sears to buy furniture for the abortion clinic they were opening in Gainesville, Florida. Avery later started a birthing center, and then in 1981 launched her most ambitious initiative: the National Black Women's Health Project, which brought worldwide attention to the specific health needs of black women. Avery received a MacArthur Foundation "Genius" Award in 1989.

Angela Davis (1944–) was a college philosophy teacher by training, yet she seemed to embody all that was threatening in the turbulent 1960s as a communist, a feminist, and a Black Panther. In 1970, she was jailed (for two years) but later acquitted on charges of conspiring in a shoot-out to free her imprisoned colleague George Jackson. Davis later wrote the classic feminist work *Women, Race, and Class* and held the Presidential Chair in African American and Feminist Studies at the University of California—the same university system, incidentally, that had dismissed her in the 1960s because of her social activism.

Wilma Mankiller (1945–) had to deal with slashed tires and death threats when she campaigned for Principal Chief of the Cherokee Nation in 1987. But Mankiller, who had already distinguished herself as an expert in community development, easily won the election. The first woman to lead a Native American tribe in modern-day America, she went on to push the tribe toward self-sufficiency.

The Guerrilla Girls formed in 1984, is a group of anonymous women who advocate for more recognition of female artists. Members hold rallies, hang posters, and speak out in public—but always disguised in gorilla masks, and they use the names of obscure dead female artists as pseudonyms. The group asks, on its Web site, "Are the Guerrilla Girls really necessary? Take a little test. On one side of a piece of paper, list all of the female artists you've heard of. On the other side of the paper, list the male artists."

YOU CAN READ

by Kathleen Odean

When I was growing up in the 1950s and '60s, I didn't have much luck finding biographies or histories about strong girls and women. True, I read all the biographies of female saints in my Catholic school library. Not only did some of them have exciting lives—and deaths—but I realized that starting a religious order or running a convent were excellent ways for women to get into management in the Middle Ages. Still, I longed for a wider range of girls and women to inspire me in my own dreams.

Today you can read about female leaders, adventurers, scientists, entrepreneurs, factory workers, pioneers, and much more. Girls and women are no longer invisible in books about the past, like they were for years. Their courage, intelligence, and hard work shine forth in these biographies and histories about remarkable girls and women who made a difference.

NO LONGER INVISIBLE: WOMEN IN HISTORY

Take a trip into the past by reading inspiring nonfiction books about girls and women breaking barriers in different times and places.

BLACK WOMEN OF THE OLD WEST

by William Loren Katz (1995).
The story of how African Americans helped settle the West, long neglected in history texts, comes alive through black-and-white photographs and prints, and fascinating accounts of African American women and their deeds. The range of their activities includes running businesses and farms, improving education, starting cultural societies, working on the Underground Railroad, and suing for their rights. This outstanding photo essay paints a richer, more accurate picture of the West than most readers will have encountered before.

28

ALL ABOUT IT!

FOUNDING MOTHERS: WOMEN OF AMERICA IN THE REVOLUTIONARY ERA

by Linda Grant DePauw. With wood engravings by Michael McCurdy (1975).
Many women had a surprising amount of freedom during the Revolutionary
period compared to the next century. DePauw delves into civic records,
newspapers, letters, and journals to piece together a rich history. Although
women had limited legal rights, the informal nature of the time led to more
opportunities than most readers would expect. Chapters detail women's roles
during the Revolutionary War, including African American and Native
American women.

GIRLS: A HISTORY OF GROWING UP FEMALE IN AMERICA

by Penny Colman (2000).
This fine overview looks at U.S. history with special emphasis on the roles
girls played from before the Colonial era to 1999. Colman frequently quotes
from girls' diaries and letters, and the memoirs of women looking back at
their childhood. Photographs and other illustrations feature girls over the
years, showing what they wore and some of their activities and jobs.

GOOD GIRL WORK: FACTORIES, SWEATSHOPS, AND HOW WOMEN CHANGED THEIR ROLE IN THE AMERICAN WORKFORCE

by Catherine Gourley (1999).
The life of a factory girl in the 1800s and early 1900s consisted of
painfully long days, unsafe surroundings, and low wages. The stories,
statistics, and pictures in this social history convey the lives of those
girls, including children as young as six. It describes how social reformers
and union activists fought to help workers improve conditions. This well-
researched book effectively documents early struggles of American girls
and women for fair treatment in the workplace.

REMEMBER THE LADIES: THE FIRST WOMEN'S RIGHTS CONVENTION

by Norma Johnston (1995).

A splendid remembrance of those great two days in the summer of 1848: the Seneca Falls women's rights convention, the beginning of a revolution that led to women getting the national vote. This history examines the background of the key players, emphasizing Elizabeth Cady Stanton and Lucretia Mott; the convention itself; and its aftermath. The author describes each day's meetings in detail and includes the entire text of the resulting Declaration of Rights and Sentiments. Photographs, a time line, and a bibliography enhance this cogent chronicle of a landmark meeting.

ROSIE THE RIVETER: WOMEN WORKING ON THE HOME FRONT IN WORLD WAR II

by Penny Colman (1995).

"Once there was a time in America when women were told that they could do anything. And they did," writes Colman about women on the home front during World War II. When working men left to fight, six million women took on new jobs, building ships and airplanes, running farms and businesses, and doing other vital work. But when the war ended, so did their jobs. This compelling history offers numerous examples of individual women's contributions to the war effort.

A SEPARATE BATTLE: WOMEN AND THE CIVIL WAR

by Ina Chang (1991).

Quotations from diaries and letters, well-chosen anecdotes, and newspaper reports give a personal dimension to this excellent history of the many roles women played on both sides of the Civil War. Using many photographs and drawings, Chang discusses the work women did as nurses, abolitionists, spies, and more, including those who disguised themselves as men to fight in both armies. An eye-opening look at nineteenth-century women.

WINNING WAYS:
A PHOTO HISTORY OF AMERICAN WOMEN IN SPORTS

by Sue Macy (1996).

A striking collection of photographs shows women participating in a variety of sports in the past, from 1886 tennis players in long skirts to a weight lifter in the 1930s. Facts and anecdotes explain how biases made it difficult for female athletes to pursue sports, while interviews and newspaper stories add a sense of immediacy. This fascinating social history will enrich the reader's understanding of how women paved the road for today's females to participate in sports.

LIFE STORIES TO INSPIRE *YOUR* FUTURE

Queens, first ladies, explorers, scientists, and civil rights activists—these are just a few of the roles played by the courageous girls and women in these biographies. How will you rock the world?

ABIGAIL ADAMS: WITNESS TO A REVOLUTION

by Natalie S. Bober (1995).

Abigail Adams's voice comes across in extensive quotations from her letters throughout this lively biography. As the wife of a Revolutionary War leader and president, John Adams, Abigail Adams, who lived from 1744 to 1818, supervised their farm and finances during her husband's frequent absences. In her letters, she urged her husband to advocate for women's legal rights, but without success. The biography combines the exciting history of the times with the compelling story of a strong woman.

AND NOT AFRAID TO DARE:
THE STORIES OF TEN AFRICAN-AMERICAN WOMEN

by Tonya Bolden (1998).

Twenty-to-thirty-page chapters describe the accomplishments of notable women, each of whom excelled in her own way. The book opens with Ellen

Craft, who courageously and cleverly escaped slavery with her husband. Others portrayed include educators Charlotte Forten Grimké and Mary McLeod Bethune, singer Leontyne Price, and writer Toni Morrison. Photographs, portraits, and quotations from the women's writings add to the impact.

ELEANOR ROOSEVELT: A LIFE OF DISCOVERY

by Russell Freedman (1993).

Eleanor Roosevelt contributed to her times in many ways: writing and public speaking; her influence on her husband, Franklin Delano Roosevelt, from his days as a New York state senator to his years as president; her service as a delegate to the United Nations; and her abiding concern for social justice and world peace. "You must do the thing you think you cannot do," she once said. This beautifully written biography, illustrated with well-chosen photographs, shows how she followed her own advice again and again, constantly growing, traveling, and undertaking new endeavors.

EXTRAORDINARY WOMEN SCIENTISTS

by Darlene R. Stille (1995).

Fifty inspiring scientists from the nineteenth and twentieth centuries come alive in short biographical sketches. Many won Nobel Prizes and other honors despite the widespread biases against women that they faced. With photographs and brief accounts of their personal lives, the essays concentrate mainly on their impressive contributions to science.

GIRLS WHO ROCKED THE WORLD: HEROINES FROM SACAGAWEA TO SHERYL SWOOPES

by Amelie Weldon (1998).

This upbeat collective biography looks at women who did something important as children or teenagers, and often continued that work as adults. It tells thirty-three stories, starting with Cleopatra and ending with tennis player Martina Hingis. In between are the stories, each with a photograph or drawing, of scientists, poets, political leaders, artists, musicians, and even a drag racer. Small sidebars offer words from today's girls about how they plan to "rock the world."

HERSTORY: WOMEN WHO CHANGED THE WORLD

edited by Ruth Ashby and Deborah Gore Ohrn (1995).

This impressive book tells the stories of 120 significant women, famous and less so, throughout history. Brief biographical sketches highlight each woman's accomplishments, quickly set her story in historical context, and point out difficulties she faced. Photographs, portraits, and sidebars add extra information. Good for browsing or as a reference book, *Herstory* revises history to include women as an important force.

IDA B. WELLS: MOTHER OF THE CIVIL RIGHTS MOVEMENT

by Dennis Brindell Fradin and Judith Bloom Fradin (2000).

This biography of the courageous Ida B. Wells describes in detail her crusade against lynching in the late 1800s and early 1900s, with painful stories of innocent victims and explicit photographs of lynchings. Born a slave, Wells became a newspaper writer and public speaker, using both roles to promote civil rights and end lynching. She also came to strongly support women's suffrage. Her willingness to speak her mind regardless of dangerous consequences makes hers an inspiring life story.

IS THERE A WOMAN IN THE HOUSE ... OR SENATE?

by Bryna J. Fireside (1994).

Jeannette Rankin, the first woman to serve in Congress, was elected in 1917 in Montana, at a time when women could vote in some but not all the states. This valuable book looks at six Democrats and four Republicans in Congress from 1917 to 1984, all of whom served as advocates for women. The chapter on each woman describes her path to a political career and her accomplishments. The result is an inspirational volume on an important topic.

RESTLESS SPIRIT: THE LIFE AND WORK OF DOROTHEA LANGE

by Elizabeth Partridge (1998).

Striking black-and-white photographs, mostly by Lange, fill the pages of this compelling story of a groundbreaking photographer. The well-written text about Lange's personal life and her career relies on primary sources, including the author's memories of Lange. This biography is notable for its honesty about the problems Lange faced balancing her children's needs and her intense drive to be a great photographer who excelled in a field dominated by men.

TEN QUEENS: PORTRAITS OF WOMEN OF POWER

by Milton Meltzer. Illustrated by Bethanne Andersen (1998).

This large, elegant book introduces ten important rulers in history from Esther to Catherine the Great, illustrated with full-page portraits and many smaller paintings. Each essay describes what is known of the monarch's childhood and rise to power, with her exploits and governing experiences set into historical context. Lesser-known women such as Boudicca and Zenobia take their places next to famous leaders such as Eleanor of Aquitaine, Isabel of Spain, and Elizabeth I of England.

WARRIORS DON'T CRY

by Melba Pattillo Beals (abridged edition, 1995).

This extraordinary autobiography chronicles the experiences of one of the nine African American students to integrate Central High School in Little Rock, Arkansas, in 1957. Beals's voice describes vividly but without bitterness the cruel reactions of some white adults and other students. She relied on emotional support from her mother and her grandmother, who once told her, "You're a warrior on the battlefield for your Lord." Beals's courage in this riveting account proves how true those words were.

WOMEN OF THE WORLD: WOMEN TRAVELERS AND EXPLORERS

by Rebecca Stefoff (1992).

Biographical sketches describe nine extraordinary Western European and American women who survived harsh conditions in their travels to Japan, Tibet, the Arctic, the Arabian peninsula, and elsewhere. Focusing mainly on the nineteenth century, the book draws on the women's writings and other primary sources, combined with photographs and maps. They climbed mountains, canoed wild rivers, rode camels, and served as spies. Portrayed as imperfect but intrepid, all are women worth meeting.

PLUNGE INTO THE PAST THROUGH NOVELS

Sometimes the best way to escape into the past is by putting yourself in the shoes of fictional girls. Join them as these strong girls come alive through their thoughts, the words they speak, the texture of their everyday lives, and their dangerous adventures.

CATHERINE, CALLED BIRDY by Karen Cushman (1994)

ESPERANZA RISING by Pam Muñoz Ryan (2000)

FREEDOM SONGS by Yvette Moore (1991)

A GATHERING OF DAYS: A NEW ENGLAND GIRL'S JOURNAL, 1830–1832
by Joan W. Blos (1979)

LETTERS FROM RIFKA by Karen Hesse (1992)

LYDDIE by Katherine Paterson (1991)

MIDWIFE'S APPRENTICE by Karen Cushman (1995)

MY NAME IS SEEPEETZA by Shirley Sterling (1992)

NUMBER THE STARS by Lois Lowry (1989)

OUT OF THE DUST by Karen Hesse (1997)

A PROUD TASTE FOR SCARLET AND MINIVER by E. L. Konigsburg (1975)

ROLL OF THUNDER, HEAR MY CRY by Mildred D. Taylor (1976)

SACAGAWEA: THE STORY OF BIRD WOMAN AND
      THE LEWIS AND CLARK EXPEDITION by Joseph Bruchac (2000)

SARAH BISHOP by Scott O'Dell (1980)

SO FAR FROM THE BAMBOO GROVE by Yoko Kawashima Watkins (1994)

STEAL AWAY by Jennifer Armstrong (1992)

THE TRUE CONFESSIONS OF CHARLOTTE DOYLE by Avi (1990)

WHO IS CARRIE? by James Lincoln Collier and Christopher Collier (1984)

THE WITCH OF BLACKBIRD POND by Elizabeth George Speare (1958)

FEMINIST WRITINGS THAT CHANGED A CENTURY

Books have always played a pivotal role in the women's movement, from being forbidden fruit to one of its main outlets for expression. Here are ten books that changed how women thought in the twentieth century.

BACKLASH: THE UNDECLARED WAR AGAINST AMERICAN WOMEN
by Susan Faludi (1991)

THE DIALECTIC OF SEX: THE CASE FOR FEMINIST REVOLUTION
by Shulamith Firestone (1970)

THE FEMININE MYSTIQUE
by Betty Friedan (1963)

OUR BODIES, OURSELVES FOR THE NEW CENTURY: A BOOK BY AND FOR WOMEN
by Boston Women's Health Collective (1970)

OUTRAGEOUS ACTS AND EVERYDAY REBELLIONS
by Gloria Steinem (1983)

A ROOM OF ONE'S OWN
by Virginia Woolf (1929)

THE SECOND SEX
by Simone de Beauvoir. Trans. and ed. H. M. Parshley. (1993; first published in France, 1953)

SEXUAL POLITICS
by Kate Millett (1970)

SISTER OUTSIDER: ESSAYS & SPEECHES
by Audre Lorde (1984)

THIS BRIDGE CALLED MY BACK: WRITINGS BY RADICAL WOMEN OF COLOR
eds. Cherrie Moraga and Gloria Anzaldua (1981)

by Magee Hickey

Women's Health Matters
Didn't Always Matter

"You've got cancer."

Those weren't the first words my doctor said to me over the phone, but almost.

First, he identified himself and then said he'd just gotten back the biopsy report after removing what I thought was a benign lump on my thyroid. It was supposed to be just a minor, little operation, for "cosmetic reasons." So minor, in fact, that since I'm a TV reporter for a women's health show, I had brought a TV camera and a producer into my operation.

"While it may not be great to have cancer," my doctor added, "this type of cancer you have is a really good one. Papillary thyroid cancer is very slow-growing and rarely spreads to other organs. You've probably had this in your neck for fifteen years and never knew it."

But still, the only words I kept hearing over and over again were "you've got cancer." I kept thinking, *How can this be happening to me?* I do stories on other people's cancer, not my own. And I do everything right, or so I thought.

At 45, I eat a balanced diet, I exercise four or five times a week,

I had just lost 15 pounds, I eat five fruits and vegetables a day, don't smoke or drink (that much!), take my calcium pills. Plus, there is no history of cancer anywhere in my family. But I, the invincible, have cancer.

So then I did what any self-respecting, tough-talking TV reporter would do. I told my doctor I'd call him back because I didn't want him to hear me crying over the phone. I had to gather my strength and get a grip before I could ask him any more questions about my "survivability rate," something I just never thought I'd be asking a doctor about myself.

To keep from crumbling, I threw myself into the history and research of thyroid problems because, if I had one, I wanted to know everything there is to know about it.

One of the first things I learned is that thyroid problems are primarily found in women and are extremely common in the United States. In fact, as of 2001, more than 20 million people were receiving treatment for thyroid disorders and two million others had a problem with their thyroids and didn't know it. And because it is usually a woman's problem, it has been misunderstood and misdiagnosed in countless cases.

Unfortunately, this is not a rare phenomenon. The history of women's health and the understanding of the female anatomy has been fraught with misconceptions and bizarre explanations, almost since the beginning of recorded time. For example, take that most female of organs, the uterus. The man recognized as the father of medicine, Hippocrates, in the fourth century B.C., believed that the uterus floated around a woman's body, not tied to any one place, and thus was responsible for all sorts of physical, mental, and moral problems. The word *hysteria* comes from the Greek word for womb, *hystera,* so the word for the surgical removal of the uterus, *hysterectomy,* and the word for a psychoneurosis of emotional excitability, *hysteria,* are forever intertwined.

Fast-forward eighteen hundred years and we find that even Leonardo da Vinci had trouble understanding the purpose of a woman's uterus. In his magnificent anatomical drawings, he shows a "milk vein" extending up to the breast, to take blood from the pregnant uterus and turn it into milk for the new born child. No wonder that three hundred years later, doctors believed that the uterus competed directly with the brain for an adequate blood supply. So that a woman who tried to develop her mind through education or a career was thought to be harming her future children in the process.

Doctors continued to be perplexed by female anatomy. In the 1840s, one of Queen Victoria's ladies-in-waiting was rumored to be pregnant because of her burgeoning belly. She was ordered to be examined by the Queen's doctor himself, who ruled she was a virgin and so he couldn't explain her swollen abdomen. She died of liver cancer shortly thereafter.

So it's not too surprising that a long time ago, doctors believed that the job of the thyroid was to fill out the hollow portions of a woman's neck in order to make it more round and beautiful. Now they know that the work of the thyroid is much more serious and vital than that. And it used to be that the only "medicine" doctors prescribed for thyroid problems was to eat a sheep's thyroid once a week. Luckily, now we have a tasteless daily pill instead.

As for the lump in my own neck, I first discovered it on television, when I was hosting a health show on the TV Food Network. My guest was a well-known endocrinologist who had just written a book about thyroid disorders. He told me that the lump in my neck, which he spotted across the TV news desk, should be examined the next morning in his office.

I followed his advice and had a fine-needle aspiration biopsy on the lump, where a few cells were removed and examined under a microscope. The report came back benign and we repeated the test for four more years. Always benign. That test, I was told repeatedly, is more than 90 percent accurate in diagnosing the most common form of thyroid cancer, which is called papillary. So I thought, *What's the hurry, I'll have the lump out eventually.*

It wasn't until I decided to do a story on thyroid problems in women for the Discovery Health show *She-TV* that I decided to have what I assumed was my benign, slow-growing lump out. Mainly, because I needed an end to my TV report. Hence, the phone call, the shock, the panic, the research.

Even though I am cancer-free now, I know I must be forever watchful for any return of the cancer tissue anywhere throughout my body. I must go to my thyroid specialist every three months for blood tests to check the thyroid levels for any signs of cancer. And I will continue doing my research, hoping, praying, and learning that when it's a woman's health issue, you must do your homework, read every book and article on the subject you can find, consult some of the great medical Web sites out there, and get fourth, fifth, and sixth opinions from a variety of doctors. The good news is that the medical establishment is finally paying more attention to women—our bodies and our minds. As more and more research is done on conditions that are unique to women, and with more and more women entering the fields of science and medicine, you and your daughters, and your granddaughters, and even your great-granddaughters, will be able to lead even healthier, more informed lives.

30

Body Politics

by Anastasia Higginbotham

My mother's mother was Roman Catholic, and she told my mom about the facts of life by referring to a line from the Hail Mary prayer. "Do you know how we say, 'Blessed is the fruit of thy womb'?" my grandmother asked my mom when she was ten. Mom nodded her head yes. "Do you know what a womb is?" she then asked. Mom shook her head no.

A discussion about body politics as they pertain to women's reproductive rights might start the same way, with the question: What is a womb? It then branches off into many directions. If the womb is bearing "fruit"—or in other words, if a woman is pregnant—is the fruit a part of the woman's own body, or is it its own thing, apart from the woman? Does it belong only to the woman, or does it half belong to the man whose sperm helped create it?

Is it nothing for a while—just a bundle of blood, tissues, and a fertilized egg—and then suddenly, it becomes something more real? A life? A child? At what point does this happen and whose business is it? Is it the woman's business, the woman's parents, the man's, the government's, or God's?

These questions have been fueling the struggle over reproductive rights for more than 200 years in this country. It comes down to one main argument: Should every woman have the legal right to make her own decisions about reproduction—whether she will have a baby and when? Some say yes, some say no. Some say it depends on a whole bunch of factors.

Reproductive rights include the right to use birth control, or contraception (the pill, condoms, or any other method a woman uses to prevent pregnancy), and the right to choose an abortion (a way of ending a pregnancy once it has begun). In order for a woman to exercise control over her reproductive life, she must have access to contraception and abortion, as well as accurate information about both, before she starts menstruating.

In the early 1800s, there was a term for the point when the fertilized egg, blood, and tissues inside a pregnant woman's womb, or uterus, becomes something more real. The term is "quickening" and refers to the moment when a pregnant woman first feels a definite stirring inside her. This tended to happen around four or five months into the pregnancy. By law, a woman could go to the doctor for an abortion up until the point of quickening, but not after.

Contraception in the 1800s was not like it is today. At that time, people believed that the only women who wanted to prevent pregnancies were prostitutes. Unmarried girls and women were expected to remain virgins until marriage, and married women were expected to have babies and to always want them. Birth control seemed unnecessary; hardly anyone was asking doctors to improve birth-control methods and abortion was legal. So that was that.

But by 1840, two things had happened. 1) Birthrates went down and it became apparent that a lot of white, married, middle-class women were choosing to have abortions, and 2) Physicians' greater understanding of fetal development changed attitudes toward quickening and abortion.

White people got especially upset about the trend of white, married, middle-class women having abortions. These women were seen by the folks in power as the right kind of women from the right kind of families who would raise the right kind of children. (If you replace the word "right" with "white" in the previous sentence, you get the full effect of the racist logic at work here.) But the truth is, all women had plenty of reasons to want to limit reproduction. They may have wanted to stay out of poverty or simply to stay alive.

Childbirth used to be extremely dangerous. It was referred to widely as "going down to death's door," and a calculation in the early 1900s showed that one of every seventeen men claimed he had a mother or sister who had died as the immediate result of childbirth. (My great-grandmother Johanna died this way.) For women who wanted to avoid this risk and/or the financial burden of many children, abortion was, they felt, a reliable option. Still, high rates of abortion among white women motivated many states to outlaw it.

Advances in medicine also led to a growing belief among physicians that "life begins at conception." The medical community became less willing to perform abortions and began advocating anti-abortion laws. By 1900, every state had an anti-abortion law of some kind.

In 1873, the Comstock Law made it illegal to "trade in, and circulate . . . obscene literature and articles of immoral use." The law applied to any sale or trade of "obscene" items within the United States and also prohibited importation of these items from other countries. Because they were believed to encourage sex just for the fun of it, contraceptive methods and advice fell under the category of obscene and immoral.

So, at the turn of the century, the deal was this: birth control and abortion were both illegal in this country. If you had sex, by choice or by force, you could get pregnant. If you got pregnant and you didn't want to be, too bad. If your pregnancy was a danger to your health, if your (illegal) method of birth control had failed, or if you had already given birth to seven kids, too bad. You were required by law to have the baby.

Then came Margaret Sanger. Working as a nurse in New York City, she saw up close the disastrous effects of women having no control over reproduction. Sanger would accompany the doctor to a house where a twenty-nine-year-old wife and mother of four was bleeding to death from an illegal abortion. This was happening in white households, African American households, first-generation Chinese, Italian, and Irish American households—no matter what their religion, politics, or economic status.

Sanger abandoned nursing to ignite public demand for legal, effective contraception. She was arrested for educating women about contraceptive methods and for smuggling boatloads of diaphragms into the country, among other things. Women working alongside Sanger went to prison, waged hunger strikes, and practically killed themselves for the right to learn about and use contraception.

So began the birth-control movement. The American Birth Control League (now Planned Parenthood Federation of America) was formed in 1921. African American organizations, such as the National Urban League, asserted strong and effective leadership in the struggle for reproductive control; smaller families meant greater economic power and freed men and women to work and remain active in the community. And a wealthy feminist named Katherine McCormick funded scientific research that led to the invention of "the Pill" in 1960—still one of the most widely used, reliable, and affordable methods of preventing pregnancy.

Here is what else you should know:

• In 1965, the U.S. Supreme Court legalized the use or prescription of birth control for married couples. Soon all U.S. states had legalized birth control for married and unmarried people.

• In 1973, the U.S. Supreme Court decided in favor of a woman's right to choose an abortion as part of her constitutional right to privacy. This is the famous *Roe* v. *Wade* decision and the origin of the term "pro-choice." Supreme Court Justice Harry Blackmun called *Roe* v. *Wade* "a step that had to be taken as we go down the road toward the full emancipation of women."

• In 1976, the Hyde Amendment said that no federal money was to be used for abortion services except when the woman can prove she was a victim of rape or incest, or that having an abortion will save her life. This was followed by numerous anti-abortion bills in the 1970s and 1980s that have made it harder and harder for poor and young women to get abortions.

• In 1992, *Planned Parenthood* v. *Casey* found that the government cannot pass laws that place "a substantial obstacle in the path of a woman seeking abortion." A "substantial obstacle" may be a law that requires a parent's or spouse's permission, mandatory waiting periods, biased information about abortion, or anti-abortion protesters gathered around the entrance to a clinic.

• Dr. David Gunn and Dr. Barnett Slepian were among those murdered during terrorist attacks on abortion clinics and providers in 1993 and 1998. Many physicians began refusing to perform abortions in response to anti-abortion terrorism or based on their own anti-abortion beliefs. By the year 2000, 86 percent of U.S. counties did not have an abortion provider.

At the start of the 21st century, the argument over women's reproductive rights is the same and yet the laws keep changing. The laws affect us all—you in your home, me in mine, and millions of other women. But as history has shown, every opinion counts and organized action brings a reaction.

So, the most important question is this: what is your opinion and what will you do about it?

31

The Making of a

DollarDiva™
(Or, How Did We Get Here???!??)

by Joline Godfrey

Madonna was one of the first female rock stars to concentrate as much on the business of her stardom as on her music. Her company, Maverick Productions, helped make her a true DollarDiva™ in the business world of rock. Celebrating herself ironically as the "Material Girl" on her 1985 video, she was well aware then of the importance of economic power and control for women.

What Madonna's songs do not do is pay tribute to her "Economic Sister Soldiers," the women who cleared the path for her to become a DollarDiva™. Do you know who those women are and why they matter to your economic power?

Do you know the events that gave you the right to get credit and own things in your own name? Do you know how it came to be that laws now require you be paid as much as your brother if you do the same kind of work? (Until 1972 you and your brother could have been hired for the same job and your employer could have legally paid him twice as much as you. Weird, but you see why Madonna and all the rest of us have a lot to be thankful for!)

Your history is not ancient and over, it's VERY recent and active—and you make it happen every day. Consider that it was just 1993 when the first National Business Plan Competition for Teen Women invited girls from across the United States to put their business dreams on paper.

Up to that point almost no one took girls seriously when it came to money and business. (Miss Teen America is a contest people take for granted—assuming EVERY girl wants to be a beauty queen. But the idea of a Ms. Business Plan winner makes a lot of people do a double take. Girls writing business plans? Starting businesses? No way!)

But since 1993, thousands of girls have entered the competition. And for millions more, the very act of THINKING about creating their own business has caused them to take themselves more seriously: considering schools, courses, and internships that support their quest for independence.

It is in many ways a heady time to be a teenage woman. Every summer now, junior high, high school, and college women all have opportunities to attend summer programs that offer skills and experiences that get them started on an economic journey. Camps for novice investors and first-time entrepreneurs give girls access to opportunities, mentors, and information historically unattainable until much later (often too late) in life.

So how did the first Business Plan Competition for Teen Women come to exist? Well, it all started a long time ago with a few real troublemakers.

You can start women's economic herstory almost anywhere in time. From the efforts of the earliest women hunters and gatherers who provided for their families, to stories of religious women who founded convents that became integral parts of working communities, to women who traveled west with husbands and fathers, only to find themselves economically on their own when the male member of the family was killed or died from disease. Early ranches, laundries, and boardinghouses were all enterprises women founded and ran to sustain themselves and their families.

But we'll start at the turn of the 20th century, in 1903, offering a few highlights of YOUR economic herstory. Keep in mind you could spend the rest of your life writing the definitive economic history of women and still not have the whole story (and I hope some of you will choose to do that!).

The list that follows is intended simply to offer a peek at some turning points in our history. The list is idiosyncratic, personal, and incomplete.

1910: Madame C. J. Walker opens her first factory.

Important because this tenacious African American woman became an inspiration for all women. Rising from a laundry worker to an economic powerhouse, Madame Walker became a role model to all women. She helped other women begin to think about and respect themselves for their own economic potential and power.

1919: Women get the vote.

Without the work of Susan B. Anthony and her sister soldiers, the suffragettes, women would not have acquired the political clout to change laws that prevented them from acquiring financial clout. At this time women were not allowed to vote, own property in their own name, or demand a fair wage equal to that of men.

1921: The Women's Bond Club of New York is founded.

At a time when few women could be found working in the financial industry, a small group of pioneers organized themselves to train and recruit more women into the field. It is today the oldest financial organization for women in the country.

1932: Frances Perkins becomes Secretary of Labor under President Roosevelt and the first woman to hold a Cabinet-level office.

This pioneer was instrumental in securing passage of the Social Security Act, unemployment insurance, and child labor legislation.

1942: Rosie the Riveter enters the workplace.

World War II sent so many men out of the country to fight that the only people left to "man" the factories making fighter planes and other essentials for the war effort were women. For the first time the country required the services of women and offered them relatively high-paying jobs to get them into the factories. Rosie the Riveter is the icon of the woman who was strong and capable, making money and providing for her family during those years.

1945: The U.S. government sends her home.

But when the soldiers began to return from Europe and Asia at the end of the war, the women were turned out of those high-paying jobs, so the men could take over again. This was a painful and humiliating time for a lot of women who had grown accustomed to the self-confidence and independence their jobs had brought them. Now they were told they were expendable: They could go back to being the "little woman," worthy of home work or the lowest-paying jobs society had to offer at the time.

1963: The Equal Pay Act passes.

Almost twenty years after women had been sent back home to take their assigned place, in an era of social change and turmoil, women found their collective voice and lobbied for the simple protection of laws that guarantee equal pay. It is these laws that make sure you and your brother are paid the same amount of money for the same work. (In 2001, girls were paid an average of $5.42 an hour; boys made $7.36 an hour in their summer jobs.)

1972: Congress passes the Equal Employment Opportunity Act.

It's fully nine years later before the next major legislation passes: equal employment opportunity. Until this act was put in place, companies routinely advertised for "girl jobs" and "boy jobs." Naturally the "boy jobs" (lawyers, doctors, machinists, managers, etc.) got higher pay. Girl jobs (secretaries, receptionists, nurses) got lower pay. Women were actually prevented from applying for a job by being told that "it isn't a job for a woman." Can you imagine?

1972: Title IX legislation enacted.

Title IX said that money spent on school-based sports must be spent equally for boys and girls. Until Title IX was passed, girls always got less money allocated for their sports activities (didn't you wonder why most colleges have big football stadiums and only big fields for girls' soccer?).

1974: Equal Credit Opportunity Act passes.

By this time, women are getting rowdy. And they're on a roll. As more women discover they can't get credit in their own name, that they can be ruined by a husband who has put them in debt, and that they have no status as a separate economic being, they get angry and organize. For better or worse, this is why you can have your own credit card today (thank your sister soldiers!!), which will allow you to establish good credit—so the banks and other institutions will see you as someone responsible enough for them to risk their money on for loans or other transactions.

1975: NAWBO incorporates.

In 1975, only about 5 percent of all businesses were owned by women (as opposed to almost 40 percent today). But those early entrepreneurs knew that if they were going to be noticed and have any economic clout, they would have to organize and talk with one another. The National Association of Women Business Owners (NAWBO) became the first "home" for women who dared to branch out on their own and start their own business.

1977: Iris Rivera, a legal secretary in Chicago, is fired for refusing to make coffee; Women Employed organize and get her job back!

Up to this point every man assumed it was the God-given role of every woman to bring them coffee in the morning. It was one of those assumed tasks that NO ONE ever questioned. Women served men coffee. The end. Until the day that Iris dared to say, NO, I won't. She made it possible for women all over the country to say, NO, I won't. The Rosa Parks of the coffee break, Iris struck a blow for all women workers.

1985: EMILY's List is born.

Early **M**oney **I**s **L**ike **Y**east. With this notion in mind, Ellen Malcolm started a fund to help finance women who wanted to run for political office but had no money to do so. With the help of EMILY's List, women began, finally, to build critical mass in the U.S. Congress.

1992: An Income of Her Own/Independent Means established.

Finally, by 1992 (that's JUST a blink of an eye historically), people began to notice that although 90 percent of ALL women will have to take care of themselves financially at some point in their lives, few of them are prepared for it. And even though many new careers and opportunities were available to women, they were still playing a game of economic catch-up because NO ONE talked to them about money when they were kids. That was the year, inspired by troublemakers who came before me (including feminist economist Marilyn Waring), I started a small project called An Income of Her Own. That simple one-day conference has since become a whole menu of programs (such as the National Business Plan Competition for Teen Women) and products developed to help girls become DollarDivas™, exploring money issues such as entrepreneurship, investing, and philanthropy.

1992: Family Leave Act passed.

Right after being elected to office, President Bill Clinton signed a law that said, in effect, women and men share equal responsibility for work and family. Finally, women cannot be fired for being pregnant or taking time off to have a child. And dads are given the right to take time off from work for child care as well. For the first time in history, companies are required by law to treat men and women in ways that recognize the dual roles of work and family, and the equal status of women and men.

1993: Take Our Daughters to Work® Day begins.

This was the year that Nell Merlino, visionary and activist feminist, realized that by giving girls a greater variety of economic role models, we could/would change their lives. Take Our Daughters to Work® Day was purposely scheduled on a schoolday (the fourth Thursday of April) so that girls would be able to promptly take their new knowledge back to the classroom. Though the program made people crazy across the land ("What about the boys?" was the battle cry of people who wanted to put a stop to the day), it caught the imagination of many women and girls (and a lot of guys and dads as well). Since that first earth-shaking day, millions of girls nationwide have "gone to work" with their parents!

1998: Springboard launched.

Though women own 40 percent of all businesses in the United States, they are able to get less than 4 percent of the total venture capital funds available. This means that though they are starting companies in record numbers, they have a MUCH harder time getting money that will allow them to GROW those companies. Determined to change this, the National Women's Business Council and the Forum for Women Entrepreneurs run a series of events that bring women business owners and potential investors together. Finally, serious investors take notice and women across the country have a shot at building BIG companies!

2001: More than 9 million women own companies.

2010: GRRL$ RULE! What will your economic herstory be?

Whenever I think about my own economic herstory, I can't help but remember the DollarDivas™ who have gone before me—making a difference, making things possible for me that were impossible for them. Among my favorites—not already mentioned—is Muriel Siebert, who in 1967 became the first woman to buy a seat on the N.Y. Stock Exchange. (No, that's not an easy chair; it's a paid membership required to do business or trade on the Exchange.)

There's also Jan Davidson (the developer of Mathblaster and a very large software company—Davidson Associates) and Oprah: two women who built fantastically large and successful businesses and who make a real contribution to community and culture as powerful philanthropists.

And topping the list is Hazel Dudley, my grandmother, who was an equal partner with my grandfather in the building of their small commercial dairy in Maine. She was a very personal and powerful economic role model for me! Every day I cherish her legacy and the lessons she passed on to me.

And I hope what you've learned right here will inspire you in the same way—perhaps to create an internship, a school project, or a summer adventure researching and creating your OWN version of your economic herstory.

32

The ERA That's Yet to Come

by Roberta W. Francis

The setting is the entrance hall of the Sewall-Belmont House, a women's rights museum and headquarters of the National Woman's Party, on Capitol Hill in Washington, D.C. A large wood and stained-glass entrance door is located stage right, and the bottom steps of a red-carpeted staircase are visible stage left. An elegantly upholstered sofa, center stage, is flanked by four white marble busts of women on pedestals, two at each end. Three of the women are attired in nineteenth-century costumes, while one statue, closest to the stairs, is dressed in a 1920s fashion.

SONIA and **ROBIN**, thirteen-year-old friends and classmates, are slumped on the sofa, waiting for SONIA's mother to finish a meeting and take them home.

ROBIN: I thought it was supposed to be over by now.

SONIA: Mom says there are always too many things to talk about.

ROBIN: My feet are so-o-o tired! But I'm glad we went on that tour through the Capitol, aren't you?

SONIA: Absolutely! It was great to see that big sculpture of those three women in the Rotunda—and then we get here and their statues are all lined up, with exactly the same faces.

ROBIN: They look so old-fashioned. It makes you realize how long ago they started the fight for women's right to vote. (*pointing beyond SONIA's head*) Which ones are there at your end?

SONIA: This one is Susan B. Anthony. I know because she has the same birthday as my mom, February 15, and Mom collects Anthony silver dollars. The pudgy one is Elizabeth Cady Stanton. Mom says she's entitled, because she had seven children. We visited her house in Seneca Falls last summer and saw lots of stuff about the first Woman's Rights Convention.

ROBIN: (*gesturing to the statue beside her*) I know this one—Lucretia Mott. My mom really likes her. She showed me an article about her being a Quaker, like us, and—what's it called?—an annal . . . an apple . . .

SONIA: An abolitionist. Like Frederick Douglass, remember? That guy who came to school and did the play about him said that after Douglass escaped, he met these women when they were all fighting against slavery, so . . .

ROBIN: Right, he worked with them to try to get equality for women, too. Cool. But who's that other statue? She looks younger and a little more modern.

SONIA: (*turning to rest her head on the arm of the sofa and closing her eyes*) We can ask Mom when she gets here, if she ever does!

ROBIN: (*curling up at the other end*) Yeah. It's starting to get dark. I can't keep my eyes open either.

(*The lights dim, then slowly come back up with a purple overtone. A young, dark- haired woman in a long-waisted white dress is standing on the bottom step of the staircase, looking intently at SONIA. SONIA glances at ROBIN, who is fast asleep, and then gets up from the sofa.*)

SONIA: Hi. Is the meeting over?

WOMAN: Meeting?

SONIA: Oh, sorry. Maybe you're here for something else.

WOMAN: True.

SONIA: (*yawning*) My mom comes in sometimes to give tours, too. Can you tell me, who's that statue next to you over there? My friend here and I were wondering.

WOMAN: (*stepping into the hall*) Alice Paul.

SONIA: Oh, right, Mom told me she lived here. Wow, imagine having a house like this, with all the fancy furniture and statues and paintings and everything.

WOMAN: It was a very different place then—a home, not a museum. Sometimes other National Woman's Party members lived here, too. Everything was much plainer. They even hung their laundry in the bedrooms upstairs. It was also their office, where they worked for women's rights, especially for the Equal Rights Amendment.

SONIA: That's the ERA, right? Mom showed my dad and my brother and me a video about it once, but I don't remember much, except that Alice Paul wrote it.

WOMAN: (*walking toward the front door and gesturing outside*) Did you see the sign on the corner? I was so glad when they put up that sign, with the

ERA's first sentence: "Equality of rights under the law shall not be denied or abridged by the United States or by any state on account of sex."

SONIA: You have it memorized?

WOMAN: It's very close to my heart.

SONIA: Have you been working here long?

WOMAN: Endlessly, it seems.

SONIA: That's like my mom says—the struggle for women's rights just goes on and on, and even when you win one thing, somebody is attacking another thing that's important for women, and there's never any time to rest.

WOMAN: (*sadly*) I wish your mother were wrong.

SONIA: She gets really excited about this stuff, though. She helped produce that ERA video.

WOMAN: Please give her my thanks.

SONIA: Do you know her—Louise Morgan?

WOMAN: No. But I've known many good women who, as you say, get excited about this stuff.

SONIA: And some of them are still working for the ERA, like Mom. It makes her really mad, because she says we shouldn't have to be fighting to put something in the Constitution that should have been there in the first place.

WOMAN: The Constitution begins with "We the people," but it has never covered men of color or any women in exactly the same way that it has protected rights for white men. Elizabeth Cady Stanton and Frederick Douglass said in 1848 that women have an equal right to vote, but it took a struggle of 72 years after that before the politicians and the country agreed.

SONIA: How could anyone say that women shouldn't be allowed to vote?

WOMAN: I could tell you dozens of reasons they gave. And some of the same arguments have been used against the ERA. But it really comes down to one thing—some people can only believe in a world where men are in charge. So they oppose the ERA because they're afraid it will take away the social and economic advantages that still go along with being male.

SONIA: But there's no good reason why women shouldn't have equal rights with men!

WOMAN: That's just what the Equal Rights Amendment is about. In 1923—only three years after the 19th Amendment finally guaranteed a woman's right to vote everywhere in the country— the ERA was written to say that all the rights in the Constitution are equal for both sexes. But as with the vote, the country wasn't ready for it.

SONIA: Maybe then, but why not now?

WOMAN: Congress didn't even pass the ERA until 1972. Then it had to be approved by 38 state legislatures within 7 years. But even though the deadline was extended, by the time it expired in 1982, only 35 states had ratified the ERA.

SONIA: You mean 15 states refused to agree that women's and men's rights should be equal?

WOMAN: I'm afraid so.

SONIA: But that was more than 20 years ago. Think of all the things women have done since then—like flying into space and becoming the Secretary of State and everything. I bet it would be easy now. Mom says if three more states vote yes, maybe there's a chance it could go into the Constitution in spite of the time limit.

WOMAN: I hope that's right. But many politicians and other people are still against it, and even some of its supporters don't think it's so important anymore. They're still discouraged after the first ERA campaign, or they mistakenly think that women have equal rights under the current laws, or they're working hard on other issues. It's what happened with the struggle for women's right to vote before we started the final national push.

SONIA: (*stepping toward the WOMAN*) We?

WOMAN: There was a big suffragist march in Washington, D.C., when Woodrow Wilson became president in 1913. Then I organized the National Woman's Party, and some of us picketed the White House and were even arrested and jailed and force-fed after we went on hunger strikes. (*putting her hand to her throat*) It was so painful!

SONIA: Were you . . . ?

WOMAN: The same thing happened with the ERA—lobbying and picketing and protests and arrests and hunger strikes—but we haven't achieved that victory yet. It will be such a glorious day, as it was with the vote in 1920, but it will also be just the beginning of the next struggle. So you always have time to put your piece into the mosaic.

SONIA: (*backing away from the WOMAN and bumping into the Alice Paul bust*) What do you mean? Who are you?

WOMAN: The struggle for women's rights is like a mosaic. Each of us puts in her small piece, and eventually we see the picture emerge. And it's a picture that is never finished. It gets larger and more detailed with each piece that is added—and more beautiful, especially when it shines and sparkles and (*her voice fading as the purple overtones in the light begin to disappear*) bears the light. . . .

LOUISE: (*entering down the stairs without looking at the WOMAN, who walks slowly up the stairway, glances back at SONIA, and disappears offstage*) Where's the light? (*turning on the switch with an audible click, filling the hall with bright white light*) Sorry I'm so late, but you could have . . . Sonia, what are you doing? Talking to that statue of Alice Paul?

SONIA: (*looking closely at the statue*) Alice Paul? . . . (*looking around confusedly*) Mom? . . . Robin? . . . Robin, wake up!

ROBIN: (*stretching and yawning*) Oh, good. I am so ready to go home.

SONIA: Robin, were you asleep the whole time? Didn't you hear that woman telling me about the ERA? She looked just like this statue of Alice Paul.

ROBIN: Are you kidding? You must have been dreaming.

SONIA: I don't think so. That was really weird. I didn't feel like I was sleepwalking.

LOUISE: Well, you're awake now. Come on, girls, time to get going!

SONIA: (*as the three exit through the front door*) Mom, that ERA video . . . can I take it to school Monday and show Mrs. Solomon? Maybe she'll play it for the class.

(*Lights fade.*)

Alice Paul

A Herstory of Language

by Judy Dothard Simmons

There is the ground. There is the air.
There is a bright light thing called Sun. It loves
A bright night thing named Moon, but we don't know that
For the long time we are very young.

We don't know to call ground Earth, that Earth is Planet, Sun is Star,
And Moon a cold, dark matter-chunk reflecting.
We learn these things and more as we experience the world;
We learn so much without reflecting, i.e., "thinking it over"
Or "giving the matter some thought," "pondering,"
"Contemplating."

The first *reflecting,* referring to Moon, is "mirroring," "bending,"
"Curving" light, Sun's light, a physicist's definition as she learns the ways
Of waves and particles and other things invisible/disguised to the naked eye.
Radio waves, reflecting off a plane in flight bounce back—
Echoes, blips on a radar screen.

Language is no simple thing. Some words and phrases, here today
Are gone tomorrow; others stay for eons, silt with nuances we
Delicately uncover: archaeologists feathering age-old dust
From fragile potsherds at *Raiders of the Lost Ark*'s snaky "dig."

History, for instance—English leafing from a French shoot off a
Latin root sprung from the Greek for knowing, to inquire,
Make an account of, which, for all we know, was a seedling in ancient Sanskrit
Or another tongue we've mostly lost the use of (it's a long story).
In 1970, around then, girls and women, some of them, took *his-story*
Literally, it being usually almost always told from a male point of view.

Women cried, "Foul!"—invented *herstory;* looks funny, sure,
Most newly coined words do, sound odd, don't feel right,
Snag on the mind (like a cat claw caught in cloth), give cause for a pause
To reflect (think over; contemplate) on *her-/his-story.*

Too much *he* and *his,* they shouted—girls and women—so much *him,* so little *her.*
She be, too! We *were,* we *are,* we *will be,* in our own right,
Girls' and women's rights, my female right; to start with, call me *Ms.*
The magazine so named began in 1972, bold move, read all about it:
Inside Ms., the book, by Mary Thom, my friend who made *herstory,*

She was really there: The Women's Movement, Women's Liberation.
Down with bras and spike heels! Up with wages, *hers* the same as *his*
For work the same or equal. Men said—more than a few—"Oh, no.
Work done by women doesn't measure up to men's, everybody knows
Naturally a *she* is less than *he.*" What awful things:
To make girls crouch so boys feel tall, and say girls can't be
Preachers, don't need college, get ahead through sex,
Mustn't run a business, can't wear the pants, or
Choose when to be mothers.

Stay in your place, men said. Who says what place is ours?
We do, said men, you're Adam's rib—made second.
Sexism, women said. Some girls run faster than a lot of boys;
Some men can't heft their weight in feathers. Some folks

Catch on quicker; some are musical, some not. You can't go by
A person's sex to know what she can do. Boys, too, play with dolls
If dads will let them. I longed for an Erector set as a little girl.

My dad was *sexist,* wouldn't let me drive his car
When I was grown and sober, but my younger brother
Drove it drunk. Dad treated his five wives like hired help
He paid in food and shelter; didn't count their feelings, thoughts,
Life-lessons learned. Obedience, they owed him:
Jump when he said, sit, fetch, heel, roll over,
Beg, like the family dog.

At least his wives weren't *battered women*: the concept
Didn't exist before the Movement made *herstory.* "Poor thing, married
To a mean drunk" was the usual comment, low-class cutting up,
But the Movement peeped some doctors, preachers, judges, too,
Who like hurting women in the name of love.

The Movement said, "A *battered woman* isn't simply weak or scared
Or lazy. She has reasons, children to protect, low skills and not much choice
Of how to make a living." Society (all of us as a whole) began to get it: *battered women*
Are a group or "class," a social problem (belonging to all of us as a whole)
Which *herstory* revealed by telling life from a female point of view.

Language validates experience, that is, gives us power to touch each other
From the inside out, and share our inner world
Of dreams, hopes, angers, hurt, deep love, and wildest joy. The Movement
Made words grow more meanings; coined new words *reflecting*
Women's situations back in the day, and way, way back before that
When words like *chairman, policeman, mailman* made it clear: No Girls Allowed!

We are! said the Movement. We can! said the girls. We will! said the women.
Some men agreed: we'll all change the world! No more titles of property—*Miss*

If a father still owned her, *Mrs.* if marriage bound her, unloved perhaps, to another man.

Ms. we are, single or married, widowed, divorced, it matters not.

We own our selves, we choose, we struggle.

Our woman-work is worthy; woman-lives leaven Wisdom.

Learn *herstory.* Balance the world!

♀ The symbol for the Roman goddess of beauty and love, Venus, and her counterpart in Greek mythology, Aphrodite. This symbol (a circle on top of a cross, signifying the spirit overcoming matter with love) has long been used to signify "female" in general, just as ♂ (a shield and spear), the symbol for the Roman god of war, Mars (and his Greek counterpart, Ares), has been used to represent "male."

BRA-BURNER: Pejorative slang for a radical feminist, derived from the myth that at the 1968 Miss America Pageant in Atlantic City, feminists burned their bras as a symbol of their revolt against the strictures society placed upon women. A group of feminists did picket the beauty pageant, and they did toss bras into a "freedom trash can" (along with other paraphernalia of traditional femininity, including girdles), but they did not rip off their own bras and burn them. The notion that a "bra-burning" had occurred spread in part because people were aware of real draft-card burnings that some anti-war activists staged in the 1960s.

CULT OF DOMESTICITY: Also known as the "cult of womanhood," this term refers to the idea that prevailed from the 1820s to 1880s of what the "ideal" or "true" woman was to be like: pious (religious in the traditional sense), chaste (a virgin until married), domestic ("a woman's place is in the home"), and submissive. Women (married or of marriageable age) who did not want to devote themselves exclusively—or at all—to being wives and mothers were deemed lost, wicked, or otherwise defective.

CULTURAL FEMINISM: The school of thought that celebrates the differences between women and men and supports the creation of a female "counterculture."

DISCRIMINATION: Unfair and almost always harmful treatment of a person or group of people because of real or perceived differences.

DISENFRANCHISE: To deny a person a right of citizenship, generally used with reference to the right to vote.

ECO-FEMINISM: The philosophy that women have a special relationship to nature and a responsibility to act as the primary caretakers of the environment.

ENFRANCHISE: To grant the rights of citizenship, especially the right to vote.

THE ERA: The Equal Rights Amendment, a proposed addition to the U.S. Constitution that would legally provide women with the same rights as men. First introduced in Congress in 1923, the ERA has yet to win formal approval.

FEMINAZI: A pejorative term coined by talk-radio personality Rush Limbaugh to describe women whom he feels are overly feminist in their leanings.

FEMININITY: A selection of qualities associated with a woman who fits society's model of what a woman should be. Characteristics traditionally associated with femininity include passivity, soft-spokenness, a nurturing nature, and being delicately dressed.

FEMINISM: The theory that women deserve an equal place in society alongside men.

FEMINIZATION OF THE WORKFORCE: A phrase that refers to the increase in the number of women who work outside the home, a trend that began during World War II.

FIRST WAVE: The group of feminists who organized the 1848 Woman's Rights Convention in Seneca Falls, New York—the first such event in American history.

GENDER: Term referring to masculine or feminine, often in the context of the differences between the two sexes.

GENDER GAP: A term coined by the National Organization of Women in 1980 with reference to the sizable difference in the way men and women vote, particularly over certain issues. The term is also used outside the context of voting, as in the case of the gap between the earnings of men and women for the same jobs.

GLASS CEILING: A metaphor for the unwritten policies and practices that prevent qualified women and people of color from reaching high-level positions, especially within corporations.

GLOBAL FEMINISM: The theory that the women of the world are one, which emphasizes the efforts to end their oppression everywhere.

GYNOCENTRIC: A female-dominated view of society, derived from the Greek word for *woman, gyne.*

HERSTORY: An alternative to "history," this word was coined to describe women's history and to call attention to the fact that women's roles in historical events were often overlooked. It is also as a reaction to male-centric terms often found in English.

HYSTERIA: From the Greek word for "of the womb," it is a disorder characterized by emotional outbreaks, excessive anxiety, and other inexplicable behavior. In the past, hysteria was seen as a female disorder (caused by some quirk of the uterus) that required that the patient be taken care of and allowed no control over her affairs. In popular usage, a woman who showed her emotions, regardless of the situation, was labeled "hysterical" and not taken seriously.

LIBERAL FEMINISM: The branch of feminism that makes full use of the government and institutions to bring about the equality of women and men.

LIBBER: See **WOMEN'S LIB.**

MALE-BASHING: Engaging in the verbal abuse of men as a group. Many feminists have engaged in male-bashing, and many who have not have been accused of it simply because they advocate equal opportunity for women or offer what they see as constructive criticism of certain attitudes and behaviors of individual men or groups of men.

MALE CHAUVINIST: A man or boy who thinks, speaks, and acts in such a way toward females as to suggest that he believes them inferior. The invective "male chauvinist pig" was popularized in the 1970s.

MARXIST FEMINISM: The theory that class struggle is the root of women's oppression.

MASCULINITY: The collection of attributes often used to describe men, such as strong, tough, strict, logical, and pragmatic.

MISOGYNY: The hatred of women.

THE "MOMMY TRACK": A pejorative term for a career path that allows a woman to balance work and family life. The idea was advanced in a 1989 *Harvard Business Review* essay, "Management Women and the New Facts of Life," by feminist Felice Schwartz, in response to the phenomenon of many mid- and upper-management women opting to withdraw from the workforce in order to spend more time raising their children. Many feminists felt that this idea set the women's movement back.

OPPRESSION: The use of power and authority to limit or deny a person or a group of people opportunities and to keep them in a state of subordination.

OTHER: Always with a capital *O,* this refers to those groups who have long been considered on the "outside" of traditional society: women, people of color, gays/lesbians/bisexual/transgendered people, and those in lower socio-economic groups.

PATRIARCHY: A social system in which males (in a family, a tribe, or a nation) have all the power and total control over the lives of females. The word derives from the Greek word for *father.*

PHALLOCENTRIC: A male-dominated view of society, from the word for the male sexual organ, "phallus."

PINK COLLAR: An area of the workforce dominated by women. The term is related to the more traditionally known blue collar, which refers to laborers, and white collar, which refers to office workers, predominantly male.

PREMENSTRUAL SYNDROME (PMS): The pain and discomfort often accompanying menstruation. Initially considered by some in the medical industry (and people at large) as a fake ailment that women used as an excuse, PMS is now much more widely accepted as legitimate and a variety of treatments are available to help ease the symptoms.

RADICAL FEMINISM: The theory that supports the total transformation or overthrow of institutions that oppress women because the existing systems could never be modified enough to wholly grant women equality with men.

SECOND SHIFT: A shorthand phrase for the fact that, unlike many working men, many working women with children actually hold down two "jobs": the one outside the home and the one inside the home. Thus, when many women come home from their wage-earning jobs, they do so only to begin a "second shift" (from helping their children with their homework and preparing dinner to doing laundry and other housekeeping chores). A single father might also work a "second shift," but the phrase is usually associated with single and married women with children.

SECOND WAVE: The feminists who organized in the late 1960s and early 1970s, which signaled a rebirth in the women's movement.

SEXISM: Discrimination based on gender.

SEXUAL HARASSMENT: Uninvited sexual advances. The term has traditionally applied to those advances being made by a person in power (for example, a boss) toward a subordinate, who might be punished (fired, demoted, or denied a promotion) for not accepting the sexual advances. Definitions of sexual harassment vary: an action or comment (or a series of such) that one person deems innocent flirtation can be, for another person, oppressive and a case of sexual harassment.

SISTERHOOD: A state of solidarity among women who have common experiences and/or goals.

SUFFRAGE: The right to vote, especially in a political election.

SUFFRAGETTE: A woman who fought for the right to vote. (**SUFFRAGIST** applies to a woman or a man who campaigned for women's right to vote.)

THIRD WAVE: The most recent revival of activity in the women's movement, starting in the mid-1980s.

WOMANIST: One who bridges the boundaries among women of color and works to unite all women, regardless of race, in the battle against sexism, while celebrating their diversity.

WOMEN'S LIB: Shorthand for the women's liberation movement, as the feminist movement of the late 1960s and early 1970s (or the Second Wave) was known. People who were active in the movement (and their supporters) were often referred to as women's libbers or libbers. Today, those terms are considered derisive.

WOMYN (WIMMON, ETC.): Much like **HERSTORY,** this is an alternative spelling of "woman" that avoids use of the "man" as part of the word, done in an effort to separate from male-dominated society and create equal status for women.

ABIGAIL SMITH ADAMS (1744–1818), born in Weymouth, Massachusetts, was one of four children of Reverend William Smith and Elizabeth Quincy Smith. Young Abigail, who had no formal schooling but was an avid reader, grew up to be a woman of formidable wit and intellect who advocated the abolition of slavery and the equality of education for girls.

At age twenty, Abigail married a lawyer from Braintree (now Quincy), Massachusetts, John Adams, who became the first vice president of the United States (1789–97) and its second president (1797–1801). Throughout her husband's political life, Abigail was a close confidante and valued counselor.

Abigail and John Adams had five children, one of whom, John Quincy Adams, had a long political career, which included serving as secretary of state (1817–25), the sixth president (1825–29), and a member of the House of Representatives (1831–48). It was as a representative that John Quincy Adams campaigned against slavery and women's exclusion from the political process (including the right to vote). Abigail, who never lived to see her son take these stands, would definitely have been proud of him, for she, no less than his father, had groomed her son for a life in politics. Abigail Adams's roughly two thousand letters that have survived are considered national treasures.

E. SUSAN BARBER teaches women's history and women's studies at the College of Notre Dame of Maryland. Among her writings are "The White Wings of Eros: Courtship and Marriage in Confederate Richmond" in *Southern Families at War: Loyalty and Conflict in the Civil War South,* edited by Catherine Clinton, and "Cartridge Makers and Myrmidon Viragos: White Working-Class Women in Confederate Richmond" in *Negotiating the Boundaries of Southern Womanhood,* edited by Janet L. Coryell, Thomas H. Appleton Jr., Anastasia Sims, and Sandra Gioia Treadway. Since 1997, Barber has been working with students at the College of Notre Dame and inmates at the Maryland Correctional Institution for Women to help raise awareness about violence against women.

ILENE "GINGY" BECKERMAN is the author and illustrator of *Love, Loss, and What I Wore*; *What We Do for Love*; and *Mother of the Bride: the Dream, the Reality, the Search for a Perfect Dress*. Her articles have appeared in *Self*, *Victoria*, and *Ladies' Home Journal*, and in the *New York Times* and the *Los Angeles Times*. She also contributed a piece called "Remember, Nobody's Perfect" to *Hands On! 33 More Things Every Girl Should Know*.

 FRITZ BESHAR has three daughters who benefit each day from Title IX. As a lawyer, athlete, and feminist, Beshar is sure that civil rights laws are a very important element of the history of this great nation. But she loves the fact that her daughters are only dimly aware of that history and can't even imagine being on the sidelines.

 SHANA COREY became hooked on women's history when she watched her first episode of *Little House on the Prairie* at age five. From then on, she read everything she could find about Olden Days girls. Imagine her surprise and delight when, years later, she went to college and discovered she could actually take classes—and get credit for learning!—about Olden Days girls! Yay, college! After college, Corey got a job editing children's books. Her first picture book, *You Forgot Your Skirt, Amelia Bloomer!*, was published in March 2000. It was named a *Publishers Weekly* Best Children's Book of 2000, a *Booklist* Editors' Choice for 2000, and a Children's Literature Choice in 2001. Corey lives in Brooklyn, New York. She has several picture books coming out in the next few years, including *Players in Pigtails* (about the All-American Girls Baseball League), which will be published in the spring of 2003.

ANN DECKER grew up in Baltimore in the 1950s and began to come of age when she went away to art school in 1967. As a child, she always loved to read illustrated books in bed and found them inspiring and magnificent. She stayed up late at night copying her favorite pictures in pencil, and that's how she learned to draw.

Decker read and drew comics and liked biographies (especially an orange-covered set with black silhouette illustrations about outstanding women). Great and beautiful women of history, like Pocahontas and Helen of Troy, were other favorite subjects for drawing. Growing older, she began to love history, books, and drawing more and more.

In 1975, Decker became a graphic artist and illustrator, working for advertising agencies, publishing companies, and left-wing organizations. Ann is now an art director at a magazine.

In 1990, she began to draw comix again and founded *Girltalk,* "the comix for your inner beast," which was published by Fantagraphics. She wrote and drew "A Tale of Three Sisters" for *Mind Riot* and "Be Careful What You Wish" for *33 Things Every Girl Should Know,* Volume 1. Decker's piece in this book is a labor of love dedicated to all those who have struggled to create something good and have not given up, ever. It is also dedicated to those who need to know these stories. You won't necessarily find out about them in school.

 OPHIRA EDUT has been an independent magazine publisher, writer, and Web developer for nearly a decade. She is the editor of *Adios, Barbie: Young Women Write About Body Image and Identity* and its expanded second edition, *Body Outlaws.* Edut is a contributing editor to *Ms.* and the founding publisher of *HUES (*Hear Us Emerging Sisters*),* an award-winning national magazine for young women of all cultures and sizes. She lives in New York City and publishes several Web sites at www.Ophira.com, including one about body image.

 FRAN ELLERS is a writer, editor, and communications consultant who works out of her home in Louisville, Kentucky. She was a newspaper reporter for seventeen years, most of them at the *Courier-Journal,* where she won state and national awards for her work. She and her husband, Mark Schaver, are the parents of a daughter, Zoe, and a son, Jack.

 ROBERTA W. FRANCIS is chair of the ERA Task Force of the National Council of

Women's Organizations, a coalition of more than one hundred groups that works to promote equality in public policy for women and girls. She was project director and script consultant for *The Equal Rights Amendment: Unfinished Business for the Constitution,* a video that premiered in 1998 in Seneca Falls, New York, as part of the celebration of the 150th anniversary of the first Woman's Rights Convention. (For more information about the seventeen-minute video, e-mail her at rfrancis@fast.net.) Francis has been a member of the board of directors of the National Woman's Party and the National Women's History Project. A former director of the New Jersey Division on Women and adjunct women's studies professor at William Paterson University in Wayne, New Jersey, she is now a gender equity consultant and writer who works primarily with Fremarjo Enterprises, Inc., on the Frederick Douglass Programs on Race Relations and Gender Equity. Residents of Chatham, New Jersey, she and her husband have two adult children, a daughter and a son. The title of the one-act she wrote for this book is "The Mosaic."

 CHARLOTTE PERKINS GILMAN (1860–1935), a leading thinker of the early women's movement, was born in Hartford, Connecticut, and raised in Rhode Island. She was one of three children born to Mary Fitch and Frederick Beecher Perkins (of the famous activist Beecher family, which included the author of *Uncle Tom's Cabin,* Harriet Beecher Stowe, and her younger sister, suffragist Isabella Beecher Hooker).

Sadly, shortly before Charlotte was born, her father abandoned his family. As a teenager, Charlotte worked at various jobs (including as a governess) to help her mother support the family. (Her limited education included a brief study at the Rhode Island School of Design.)

At age twenty-four, Charlotte married artist Charles Stetson. After the birth of their daughter in 1885, Charlotte suffered severe depression for which a prominent physician, Dr. S. Weir Mitchell, prescribed absolute rest. This experience was the inspiration behind her now classic horror story "The Yellow Wallpaper." (She divorced Stetson in 1894, giving him custody of their daughter, and moved to San Francisco. In 1900, she married her first cousin, lawyer George Gilman.)

Charlotte Perkins Gilman's other works include a collection of poems, *In This Our World* (1893), *Women and Economics* (1898), *Concerning Children* (1900), *The Home* (1903), *Human Work* (1904), and the short story "Herland" about a female utopian society. "Herland" appeared in a 1915 edition of the *Forerunner,* a feminist magazine founded by Gilman in 1909. It was also in 1915 that she, along with Jane Addams, Florence Kelley, Belle La Follette, Fanny Garrison Villard, Emily Balch, Jeannette Rankin, Lillian Wald, Crystal Eastman, Carrie Chapman Catt, and a host of other movers and shakers, founded the Woman's Peace Party. Gilman's autobiography, *The Living of Charlotte Perkins Gilman,* written in the mid-1920s, was published in 1935, shortly after she died.

 JOLINE GODFREY is the CEO of Independent Means Inc. (www.independentmeans.com). Her books include *Twenty $ecrets to Money and Independence: The DollarDiva™'s Guide to Life* and *No More Frogs to Kiss: 99 Ways to Give Economic Power to Girls.* She lives in California and works with girls and women everywhere to create economic opportunity for the next generation of DollarDivas™.

 ELISABETH GRIFFITH has served as headmistress since 1988 of the Madeira School, an independent residential and day school for girls in grades nine through twelve in McLean, Virginia. At the time of her appointment, she was working on a major historical study of the Equal Rights Amendment from 1923 to 1983. Her research was funded by the prestigious J. Franklin Jameson Fellowship, awarded by the American Historical Association and the Library of Congress. In honor of her tenure, the Madeira board of directors created the Elisabeth Griffith Women's Leadership Lecture Series, which was launched in May 1999 by First Lady Hillary Rodham Clinton.

Griffith, who earned a B.A. from Wellesley College, an M.A. from Johns Hopkins University, and a Ph.D. in history from the American University, belongs to the Society of American Historians, is listed in the Directory of American Scholars, and currently serves on the advisory board of the White

House Project, a bipartisan effort to create support for a woman president.

In 1999, Griffith served as a consultant for Ken Burns's PBS documentary *Not for Ourselves Alone,* about Elizabeth Cady Stanton and Susan B. Anthony. This documentary was based in part on Griffith's book *In Her Own Right* (1984), a biography of Stanton, which was chosen as one of "the 15 best books of 1984" and one of the "Books of the Century" by the editors of *The New York Times Book Review.*

Griffith is married to John Deardourff, a retired political consultant and media strategist. They are the parents of Megan (Duke '99) and John David (Taft '04). She has two grown stepdaughters, Anne and Katie.

 NANCY GRUVER is founder and publisher of the groundbreaking international publications *New Moon®: The Magazine for Girls and Their Dreams* and *New Moon® Network: For Adults Who Care About Girls.* You can learn more about New Moon®—including about the four New Moon® books and the girl-run television show *Shoot for the Moon*—at www.newmoon.org.

Gruver's and New Moon®'s numerous honors include the 2001 Anne Bancroft Award, the "Women of Distinction" award from the National Association for Women in Education, the NOW "Young Feminists Making a Difference" award, and the Feminist Majority Foundation's "Feminist of the Year" Award. New Moon®'s girl editors were named winners of the Center for Women's Policy Studies' Jessie Bernard Wise Women Award (1995). Additionally, *New Moon®* magazine has garnered six Parents' Choice Foundation Awards, five Educational Press Association of America Design and Editorial Awards, and the *Utne Reader*'s 1994 Alternative Press Award.

Gruver is also founder of Girls International Forum, a nonprofit group that educates people about girls' issues. In 1995, she organized a delegation of thirteen American girls to attend the United Nations Fourth World Conference on Women in Beijing, China.

Born in Philadelphia, Gruver grew up in New York and Connecticut, earning a B.A. from Connecticut College and an M.P.A. from Harvard University. She lives in Duluth, Minnesota, with her husband and loves e-mailing her daughters at college.

SUHEIR HAMMAD is the author of the volume of poetry *Born Palestinian, Born Black* and the prose memoir *Drops of This Story.* Her poetry and prose have appeared in several anthologies and journals, and her column "Psalm 26:7" in *STRESS* magazine is the longest-running column written by a woman in any hip-hop publication.

 SAFIYA HENDERSON-HOLMES (1950–2001) was a native New Yorker who grew up in the Bronx. After earning a B.S. in physiotherapy from New York University, she worked at Harlem Hospital as a physical therapist and also served as a natural-birthing coach on the side. A love of literature prompted her to earn an M.F.A. in creative writing from New York's City College in the 1980s. Thus began her second career as a writer, performance artist, and educator (she was a professor of creative writing at Syracuse University at the time of her death).

Henderson-Holmes's works include the collections of poetry *Daily Bread* and *Madness and a Bit of Hope* (which contains "rituals of spring"); the plays *I'll Be Home Soon* and *Testimony;* and the anthology (co-edited with Ellen J. Goldman) *Racing and (E)Racing Language: Living with the Color of Our Words.* Her poetry and fiction have appeared in an array of periodicals and anthologies, and her many honors include the Poetry Society of America's William Carlos Williams Award, the Fannie Lou Hamer Award from Medgar Evers College, numerous Pushcart Prize nominations, and several fellowships from the New York Foundation for the Arts. Henderson-Holmes was in search of a publisher for her series of narratives *"C"ing in Colors,* which was born of her struggle with a rare form of cancer, when she died on April 8, 2001.

 MAGEE HICKEY spent fifteen award-winning years covering local news in New York City. During her ten years at WNBC-TV, she was the first anchor of the highly successful *Weekend Today in New York* newscast. Hickey also won an Emmy in 1992 for investigative journalism for her yearlong reports on problems in the New York City Emergency Medical Services. She gained an impressive reputation as a tenacious investigative reporter and a resourceful general assignment reporter who can handle any kind of story or interview. In recent years, Hickey has focused on health issues for women in their thirties and forties and on child care. In 1999, she hosted two weekly shows on Cablevision's MetroGuide channel: *Out with the Kids* and *Real Women*. In 2000, she became a correspondent for the Discovery Health show *She-TV*. Magee Hickey is married and is the mother of two daughters.

 ANASTASIA HIGGINBOTHAM writes from her home in Brooklyn, New York. She works with the girls' rights advocacy organization Girls Incorporated and contracts with other nonprofits that are devoted to improving kids' and women's lives. Higginbotham has written for *Glamour*, *The Women's Review of Books*, *Nerve*, *Ms.*, and the anthology *Listen Up: Voices from the Next Feminist Generation*.

 COLINE JENKINS-SAHLIN, a.k.a. "the woman with a cause," is the president of the Elizabeth Cady Stanton Trust, which in August 2000 purchased a national treasure—three thousand objects from the women's rights movement, dating from 1840–1970. The trust's mission is to blast the knowledge of these objects and their essential American history into the consciousness of American citizens (and Jenkins-Sahlin solicits *your* help in this mission). In the late 1990s, Jenkins-Sahlin was intensely involved in the successful nationwide campaign to install, for the first time ever, a statue of a woman (the suffragette statue) into the Rotunda of the U.S. Capitol. Jenkins-Sahlin, ever busy, holds an elective office in the Greenwich (Connecticut) town legislature, serves as a board member of the National Museum of Women's History, and works as Connecticut chapter chair of the Friends of the Women's Rights National Park in Seneca Falls, New York. As a television producer (Third Wave TV), she has co-produced six documentaries, all of which empower women. This indefatigable great-great-granddaughter of Elizabeth Cady Stanton lives in Old Greenwich, Connecticut, with her husband, Gunnar, and their children, Elizabeth and Eric. Jenkins-Sahlin thanks writer Jana Siciliano for her help with her essay "The Women's Declaration." Special thanks to Vivien Rose and Jamie Wolfe at the National Historical Park for Women's Rights, Seneca Falls, New York.

ELIZABETH JOHNSON is a poetic daydreamer who is currently working on a degree in design at Cornish College of the Arts in Seattle. Elizabeth has been writing down her imagination for many years and has been honored by being published in literary magazines and representing Seattle poetry in the NAACP ACT-SO competition. The title of the poem that Johnson wrote for this book is "Herstory."

 NORMA JOHNSTON, who also writes as Nicole St. John, Kate Chambers, Catherine E. Chambers, Lavinia Harris, Pamela Dryden, Elizabeth Bolton, and Adrian Robert, is the author of more than ninety works, among them the acclaimed *Keeping Days* series and the biographies of Louisa May Alcott and Harriet Beecher Stowe. Her latest book is *Feather in the Wind,* a supernatural suspense story. Her Web site is www.ChipmunkCrossing.com; her e-mail, johnstonstjohn@worldnet.att.net.

 KATHLEEN KRULL lives in San Diego with her husband, artist Paul Brewer. She is the author of *Lives of Extraordinary Women: Rulers, Rebels . . . And What the Neighbors Thought; Wilma Unlimited: How Wilma Rudolph Became the World's Fastest Woman;* and other biographies for young readers. Find out how nosy she is (and play the "Extraordinary Women, Extraordinary Trivia" game) at www.kathleenkrull.com.

 BETSY KUHN is the author of *Angels of Mercy: The Army Nurses of World War II; Not Exactly Nashville* (a novel); and *Top Ten Jockeys,* about Thoroughbred-horse jockeys. She lives in Maryland with her husband, twin sons, and her pet Volkswagen, a 1971 Super Beetle named Herb. She thanks Flo Smith, Bethena Moore, Donna Graves, Greg, her mom, and everyone else who helped with the essay she wrote for this book.

 SUE MACY has loved American history since elementary school. She couldn't help but imagine what life was like in the times she read about in her textbooks, even when those books focused on politics and only mentioned men. When she entered Princeton University, she learned that women made history, too, and wrote papers about early women tennis champions, female social reformers, and the struggles of immigrant girls and women in New York City. A former editor of magazines for children and young adults and the editor-in-chief of the *Scholastic Children's Dictionary,* Macy is now a full-time writer, editor, and publishing consultant. Her books include *A Whole New Ball Game: The Story of the All-American Girls Professional Baseball League; Winning Ways: A Photohistory of American Women in Sports; Play Like a Girl: A Celebration of Women in Sports* (edited with Jane Gottesman); *Girls Got Game: Sports Stories & Poems* (editor and contributor); and *Bull's-Eye: A Photobiography of Annie Oakley.*

 ROSALIE MAGGIO, author of seventeen books for young people and adults, read more than eight thousand books to find quotations for *The New Beacon Book of Quotations by Women.* She is on the advisory board of *New Moon Network: For Adults Who Care About Girls,* has been part of the movement to replace sexist language with sensible, everyday nonsexist language (firefighter, not fireman, for example), and has written a biography in French about the amazing woman they called "The Fiancée of Danger," Marie Marvingt.

 PATRICIA C. McKISSACK (along with husband and co-author, Fredrick McKissack) has written more than seventy-five fiction and nonfiction books for young readers. Her *The Dark-Thirty: Southern Tales of the Supernatural* is a Newbery Honor Book, and she also wrote *Mirandy and Brother Wind,* a Caldecott Honor Book, illustrated by Jerry Pinkney. McKissack is a 1964 graduate of Tennessee State University with a bachelor's degree in English and a master's degree from Webster University in early childhood education. She and her husband live and work in Chesterfield, Missouri, a suburb of St. Louis.

 NOMAS is the oldest pro-feminist men's organization in the United States. It was started in 1975 when a group of men who were enrolled in a women's studies course at the University of Tennessee held what they announced as "The First National Conference on Men and Masculinity" (M&M) in Knoxville, Tennessee. In 1981, after five successful M&Ms around the country, the National Organization for Changing Men (NOCM) was established as the national sponsoring body to ensure the continuation of the M&Ms. The name was changed to the National Organization for Men Against Sexism (NOMAS) in 1990. In 2000, NOMAS celebrated its silver anniversary with the 25th M&M in Colorado Springs, Colorado, and through a re-visioning process has committed to continuing M&Ms for the foreseeable future. NOMAS continues to bring together men and women to work for gender equality and social justice for everyone. More information is available at www.nomas.org.

 KATHLEEN ODEAN, a children's librarian for seventeen years, is the author of *Great Books for Girls: More than 600 Books to Inspire Today's Girls and Tomorrow's Women; Great Books for Boys: More than 600 Books for Boys 2 to 14;* and *Great Books About Things Kids Love.* She has served on the Newbery and Caldecott Award committees and as chair of the 2002 Newbery Award Committee. She lectures nationally on children's books and is a contributing editor to *Book: The Magazine for the Reading Life.* Odean lives in Barrington, Rhode Island, with her husband.

 ANN POWERS started writing about rock as a screaming teenage new waver in Seattle at the dawn of the 1980s. She never stopped, although she tried. By now she's authored a book, *Weird Like Us: My Bohemian America,* co-edited the anthology *Rock She Wrote: Women Write About Rock, Pop, and Rap,* and written for many publications, big and little. These days, she gets paid by the *New York Times* to go to concerts and send back reports from the front. When she's not busy losing more of her hearing, she hangs out in Brooklyn, New York, with her mate, Eric Weisbard, and listens to much more music than others think humanly possible—and still doesn't get to every record in the pile.

 JUDY DOTHARD SIMMONS is an award-winning poet, columnist, feature writer, editor, and broadcaster. Her work appears in www.Africana.com, *Essence, Ms., The Crisis, QBR, The Black Book Review,* and other periodicals and has been anthologized in *Wild Women Don't Wear No Blues, Confirmation, Giant Talk, Drum Voices, New Rain #7,* et al. She lives in Anniston, Alabama.

 NATASHA TARPLEY is the author of the family memoir *Girl in the Mirror: Three Generations of Black Women in Motion* and the editor of the anthology *Testimony: Young African-Americans on Self-Discovery and Black Identity.* She has also written several books for children, including the award-winning *I Love My Hair!* and *Bippity Bop Barbershop!* Tarpley is the recipient of a National Endowment for the Arts Fellowship. Her work has been widely anthologized and taught around the world. She currently lives in New York City.

 M. CAREY THOMAS (1857–1935), who grew up in Baltimore, Maryland, was one of several children born to James Carey Thomas, a physician, and Mary Whitall Thomas, who, along with her sister, Hannah Whitall Smith, was active in the Woman's Christian Temperance Union (WCTU).

A lifelong intense advocate for girls' opportunity for a quality education (from primary school on up), Thomas is best remembered as the driving force behind the development of Bryn Mawr into one of the finest American colleges in her roles as professor of English (1885–94), dean (1885–1908), and eventually, as president (1894–1922). Thomas, a passionate suffragist, became, in 1908, the first president of the National College Women's Equal Suffrage League. She was also a central figure in the National American Woman Suffrage Association and a staunch supporter of the National Woman's Party and its campaign for the Equal Rights Amendment. Thomas, who never married, is also remembered for her opposition to marriage and her position that marriage should not preclude a woman from having a career.

PAULA A. TRECKEL is a professor of history at Allegheny College in Meadville, Pennsylvania. She enjoys teaching courses on American women's history and educating young women and men about how important the feminist movement has been in shaping their lives. She has published many articles on American women's history and delivered an address celebrating the 75th anniversary of women's right to vote at the Chautauqua Institution in New York. She is the author of *To Comfort the Heart: Women in Seventeenth-Century America* and is writing a book entitled *Dearly Beloved: The Romance and Ritual of American Weddings.* She has also appeared as a contestant (and won!) on the History Channel's *History I.Q.* game show.

 MARSHA WEINSTEIN lives in Prospect, Kentucky, where she spends her time as a social activist. Her philosophy is that little girls with dreams become women of vision and action. Women's history and girl leadership development are her passions. She is founder of the Alliance for Girls and co-founder of the Elizabeth Cady Stanton Trust. She co-founded and is the chair of the board of directors of Youthbuild Louisville. While serving on the national board of directors of the Girl Scouts of the USA, Weinstein chaired their communications and public policy committee. As the former executive director of the Kentucky Commission on Women, she is most proud of her work with former governor Brereton Jones. She convinced him to grant clemency to nine domestic violence victims who had been incarcerated for killing or attempting to kill their abusers.

ABOUT THE EDITOR

 TONYA BOLDEN, the editor of the first book in the 33 Things series, *33 Things Every Girl Should Know* (an ALA Best Book for Young Adults), has more than a dozen books published for children, teens, and adults. Her other books include *And Not Afraid to Dare: The Stories of Ten African-American Women; Strong Men Keep Coming: The Book of African American Men; Rock of Ages: A Tribute to the Black Church* (illustrated by R. Gregory Christie); and *Tell All the Children Our Story: Memories and Mementos of Being Young and Black in America.* At schools, libraries, and other venues, Bolden frequently holds readings, gives talks, and conducts workshops on the wonders of history, the joys of reading, and the power of the written word. To learn more about her work, visit www.tonyabolden.com.

ACKNOWLEDGMENTS

We gratefully acknowledge the following for permission to use their work in this book.

E. Susan Barber for "Time Matters." Copyright © 2002 by E. Susan Barber. Used by permission of the author.

Ilene Beckerman for "Life Is Sometimes a Fashion Parade." Copyright © 2002 by Ilene Beckerman. Used by permission of the author.

Fritz Beshar for "Title IX Helped Level the Playing Field." Copyright © 2002 by Fritz Beshar. Used by permission of the author.

Shana Corey for "What Women Did Before NOW" Copyright © 2002 by Shana Corey. Used by permission of the author.

Ann Decker for "'Don't Agonize, Organize!'" Copyright © 2002 by Ann Decker. Used by permission of the author.

Ophira Edut for "Beauty Can Be a Beast." Copyright © 2002 by Ophira Edut. Used by permission of the author.

Fran Ellers for "The Roll Call of Crusaders." Copyright © 2002 by Fran Ellers. Used by permission of the author.

Roberta W. Francis for "The Mosaic." Copyright © 2002 by Roberta W. Francis. Used by permission of the author.

Joline Godfrey for "The Making of a DollarDiva™ (Or, How Did We Get Here???!??)." Copyright © 2002 by Joline Godfrey. Used by permission of the author.

Elisabeth Griffith for "The 'Representing.'" Copyright © 2002 by Elisabeth Griffith. Used by permission of the author.

Nancy Gruver for "Women Weren't Always in the Books." Copyright © 2002 by Nancy Gruver. Used by permission of the author.

Suheir Hammad for "U.S. Women Are Diverse." Copyright © 2002 by Suheir Hammad. Used by permission of the author.

Safiya Henderson-Holmes for "rituals of spring" from *Madness and a Bit of Hope* by Safiya Henderson-Holmes. Copyright © 1990 by Safiya Henderson-Holmes. Used by permission of the author.

Magee Hickey for "Women's Health Matters Didn't Always Matter." Copyright © 2002 by Magee Hickey. Used by permission of the author.

Anastasia Higginbotham for "Body Politics." Copyright © 2002 by Anastasia Higginbotham. Used by permission of the author.

Page 9: by Paul Stahr for the National Suffrage Publishing Company, © Life Publishing Company. Page 12: portrait of Abigail Adams by Benjamin Blyth courtesy of the Massachusetts Historical Society. Page 17: courtesy of the Elizabeth Cady Stanton Trust. Pages 28–43: courtesy of Melia Donovan. Pages 44–45, 49, 50, 52–53, 102, 103, 142, 205: courtesy of the Library of Congress. Page 70: photograph of Sacagawea statue (top) courtesy of the North Dakota Tourism Department; photograph of Wendover (bottom left) courtesy of the Frontier Nursing Service, Wendover, Ky.; photograph of Mary McLeod Bethune Memorial (bottom right) courtesy of the Elizabeth Cady Stanton Trust. Page 71: photograph of Maria Mitchell House (top) courtesy of the Maria Mitchell Association; photograph of Alva Smith Vanderbilt Belmont Mausoleum (bottom) courtesy of the Woodlawn Cemetery. Page 72: photograph of Rosie the Riveter Memorial (left) copyright © Lewis Watts; photograph of "Ivy Green" (right) courtesy of the Helen Keller Birthplace, copyright © Patrick Hood. Pages 98–99, 100, 104, 109: courtesy of the National Archives. Pages 114, 137: copyright © Hulton/Archives / Getty Images. Pages 130–35: courtesy of John Clemente, from *Girl Groups: Fabulous Females That Rocked the World*, copyright © 2000. Page 133: courtesy of John Clemente, copyright © Rosalind Ashford Holmes. Page 163: courtesy of Fahey/Klein Gallery, copyright © Steve Schapiro. Page 167: courtesy of the Bancroft Library, University of California, Berkeley. Page 185: courtesy of Magee Hickey.

MANA, 90
Mankiller, Wilma, 10, 160, 175
Maria Mitchell House, 71
Marine Corps Women's Reserve (WR), 99, 100
Married Women's Property Act, 51, 151
Martha and the Vandellas, 132
Martin, Del, 157
Maverick Productions, 193
McCall's, 118
McCarthy, Joe, 113
McClintock, Elizabeth W., 16
McClintock, Mary Ann, 16, 49
McClure's, 81
McLachlan, Sarah, 160
McLaughlin, Mignon, 68
Medical College of Pennsylvania, 152
Medicine Eagle, Brooke, 66
Men Against Domestic Violence, 167
Men Against Pornography, 167
menstruation, 189
Merlino, Nell, 198
Mille, Agnes de, 88
Miller, Albert, 144
Millett, Kate, 165, 184
Ming-Na, 10
Mink, Patsy, 113, 114
Mississippi Freedom Democratic Party (MFDP),
    158
Mitchell, Maria, 71
Modern Woman: The Lost Sex (Farnham and
    Lundberg), 157
Monroe, Marilyn, 11
Moore, Bethena, 101, 102–103
Moreno, Rita, 10
Morgan, Louise, 202
Morgan, Robin, 84, 165
Morris, Esther Hobart, 168
Morrison, Toni, 180
Mother Earth, 79
Mott, James, 167
Mott, Lucretia, 15–16, 20, 21, 47, 84, 162,
    167, 169, 178, 200
Mount Holyoke College, 86, 151
Ms., 158, 164, 207
MTV, 120
muckraking, 81
Mullaney, Kate, 71, 171
Muller v. Oregon, 155
Murray, Judith Sargent Stevens, 150
museums, women's, 73

N

National Aeronautics and Space Administration
    (NASA), 141–142

National Alliance Opposed to Woman Suffrage
    (NAOWS), 155
National American Woman Suffrage Association
    (NAWSA), 84, 154, 156
National Archives for Black Women's History,
    89
National Asian Women's Health Association, 90
National Association of At-Home Mothers, 90
National Association of Colored Women, 87,
    89, 154, 171, 172
National Association of Colored Women's Clubs
    (NACWC), 87
National Association of Women Business
    Owners (NAWBO), 197
National Black Women's Health Project, 90,
    175
National Business Plan Competition, 194, 197
National Coalition Against Domestic Violence,
    90
National Consumers League, 80
National Council of Jewish Women (NCJW), 86,
    154
National Council of Negro Women, 71, 89, 172
National Federation of Afro-American Women,
    86, 87
National Federation of Business and
    Professional Women's Clubs, 89
National Federation of Women's Clubs, 154
National Leadership Conference of Women
    Religious, 159
National League of Colored Women, 89
National Organization for Men Against Sexism
    (NOMAS), 167–168
National Organization of Women (NOW), 84,
    90, 164
National Register of Historic Places, 69
National Urban League, 190
National Woman Suffrage Association (NWSA),
    51, 84, 152, 153, 154
National Woman's Party, 69, 84, 155, 156,
    200, 201, 203
National Women's Air Derby, 89
National Women's Business Council, 198
National Women's History Project, 159
National Women's Political Caucus, 90, 174
National Women's Trade Union League
    (NWTUL), 87
National Youth Administration, 106
Native Americans, 13, 54, 55, 59, 62, 70,
    160, 175, 180
Navy Women's Reserve (WAVES), 100, 157
"New Colossus, The" (Lazarus), 69
New England Magazine, The, 28
New Look, 118

Violence Against Women Act II, 160
"Voice from the South by a Black Woman from
    the South, A" (Cooper), 172

W

Wakatsuki, Jean, 157
Wald, Lillian, 80
Walker, A'Lelia, 70
Walker, Alice, 165
Walker, Dr. Mary Edwards, 144
Walker, Madame C. J., 70, 195
Walker, Maggie Lena, 143
Walker Building, 70
War Department, 102
Waring, Marilyn, 198
Washington, George, 10, 11, 13
Washington, Margaret Murray, 154
Weber, Lois, 144–145
Wellesley College, 86
Wells-Burnett, Ida B., 81, 146, 154, 181
Wendover, 70
West, Cornel, 167
Wheatley, Phyllis, 10
WHER, 157
Whitney, Eli, 150
Wilder, Laura Ingalls, 54
Willa Cather Pioneer Memorial, 70
Willard, Emma Hart, 151
Willard, Frances, 153, 171
Wilson, Heather, 113
Wilson, Woodrow, 172, 173, 203
Winnemucca, Sarah, 146
Wittenmeyer, Annie, 153
Wolf, Naomi, 166
Wollstonecraft, Mary, 150
Woman Suffrage Amendment, *see* Nineteenth
    Amendment
womanist, *see* feminism, womanist
Woman's Bible, The (Stanton), 154
Woman's Era Club, 86
Woman's Home Companion, 122, 125
Woman's Peace Party, 154
womb, *see* uterus
women:
    African American, *see* African American women
    Asian, *see* Asian women
    books about, 176–184
    clothing of, *see* clothing
    education of, 14, 19, 22, 23–27, 49, 51,
        71, 74, 82, 170, 172, 207
    health of, 51, 85, 88, 90, 174–175, 185–188
    Latina, *see* Latina women
    magazines of, *see* magazines, women's
    money and, 142; *see also* women, property

    rights of; women, wages of
    as musicians, 130–135
    pioneer, 54–61, 176
    property rights of, 14, 19, 22, 47, 48, 49,
        51, 151, 193, 196–197
    quotes by, 65–68
    religion and, 19, 154, 159
    in science, 180
    and sports, 136–139, 140–141, 179, 196;
        see also Title IX
    suffrage of, *see* suffrage, women's
    violence against, 88, 122, 168, 208–209
    wages of, 14, 19, 47, 51, 75, 87, 107,
        113, 153, 158, 170, 171, 177, 193,
        195, 196, 207
    working, 19, 49, 74, 75, 77, 87, 99–103,
        107, 151, 169, 171, 173, 177, 193–199
Women, Race, and Class (Davis), 175
Women Airforce Service Pilots (WASPs), 100,
    157
Women Employed, 197
Women's Armed Service Integration Act, 103
Women's Army Corps (WACs), 100, 156, 175
Women's Bond Club of New York, 195
Women's Christian Temperance Union
    (WCTU), 153, 171
Women's Educational and Industrial Union
    (WEIU), 85
Women's League, 75
women's liberation movement, 164, 166, 207
Women's Rights Project, 174
Women's Sports Foundation, 90
women's studies, 146–149, 158
Women's Trade Union League (WTUL), 154, 155
Woodhull, Victoria, 153
Woodward, Charlotte, 45–51
World Conference on Women, 166
World War I, 79, 80, 82, 105, 117, 124, 128, 142
World War II, 99–102, 105, 118, 124, 143,
    157, 163, 164, 175, 178, 195, 196
Wright, Martha Coffin, 49

Y

Yale Women's Crew, 138
"Yellow Wallpaper, The" (Gilman), 28–43, 88
Young Women's Christian Association (YWCA), 85
Younger, Maud, 172–173

Z

Zaharias, Babe Didrikson, 137, 156
Zenobia, Queen, 182
Zurich, University of, 27